TIME OUT FOR GINGER

photo by Fred Fehl

Time Out for Ginger

COMEDY IN THREE ACTS
by

RONALD ALEXANDER

DRAMATISTS PLAY SERVICE · INC.
New York

TIME OUT FOR GINGER *was first produced by the Alley Theater in Houston, Texas. It was produced in New York by Shepard Traube and Gordon Pollock in association with Don Hershey at the Lyceum Theater on November 26, 1952. Scenery and lighting were by Eldon Elder, and the play was directed by Shepard Traube. The cast was as follows:*

LIZZIE, the maid .... Laura Pierpont
AGNES CAROL .... Polly Rowles
HOWARD CAROL .... Melvyn Douglas
JOAN, their daughter, age 18 .... Mary Hartig
JEANNIE, their daughter, age 16 .... Lois Smith
GINGER, their daughter, age 14 .... Nancy Malone
EDDIE DAVIS, an athlete; Joan's boy friend .... Conrad Janis
TOMMY GREEN, Ginger's boy friend .... Larry Robinson
MR. WILSON, the high school principal .... Roland Wood
ED HOFFMAN, bank president, Howard Carol's boss...Philip Loeb

Synopsis of Scenes

ACT I

The living-room of the home of Mr. and Mrs. Howard Carol. Early Fall, 4:30 one afternoon.

ACT II

Scene 1.   Four weeks later.
Scene 2.   A Saturday afternoon. Four weeks later.

ACT III

The same evening.

ACT ONE

The scene is the home of Mr. and Mrs. Howard Cecil, upper middle-class residents of a typical American town or small city. The living-room, where the action passes, is bright, cheery, and roomy. At the back of the stage, above the living-room proper, is the entrance hallway, which runs from about Center-stage to the extreme Right. At extreme Right of this hallway, up-stage, is the front door, unseen by the audience. This door is heard slamming each time anyone uses it, and each time the door-bell is heard when anyone wants to enter. Just visible to the audience, to the Left of the unseen front door is a small clothes-closet, in the up-stage wall of the set, and coats, hats, and the like, are perceived when the door opens. The hallway extends to the Left about half-way across the upper part of the stage. Standing near the wall are, immediately to the Left of the clothes closet door, a chair and Left of that an oblong table, with flowers or a potted plant on it. A flight of stairs, about Center stage, comes down (presumably) from the second floor. The actors enter from what is supposed to be the top of the stairs, unseen by the audience. Three or four steps below the entrance to the stairway is a small landing, from which the lower two or three steps, down to stage level, turn to stage Right. These last steps are provided with a banister, and two newel posts form the extremities of the stairway. The Right wall of the stage, starting from below where the invisible front door is supposed to be, and somewhat to its Left, is a large window, a bit over half-way down-stage. Below this, not far from the curtain-line, is a radio-console. A small mirror hangs on the wall over it. Against the up-stage wall, Left of the bottom of the stairway, is a flat-topped sideboard, in which is at least one drawer. A wastebasket stands nearby. To the Right of the sideboard, a little below the stairs, is a small phone table with a phone on it. Small chairs to R. and L. of the phone table. The

Left wall of the room includes the door to the kitchen, preferably a swinging door. Just below this, against the wall, a small table, with a lamp and a few framed family photos. Below this is a corner, described hereafter as D.L. corner. On two sides of this, facing the audience, are bookshelves, some of which have a few books, and one of which has bottles, cans, jars, paintbrushes. A little further down-stage to the Left is a bench, in which is a practical drawer or lift-top. Standing out a little from this corner is a small work table, described hereafter as Ceramic Table; on this a small potter's wheel. A few prints and small pictures on the walls of the corner. At the extreme down-stage extremity of the corner is a small chair, described as a child's chair. Above the window at stage Right is a jog in the room formed by part of the set; this masks the Right extremity of the hallway leading to the front door. In this jog is a small table, on which is a lamp. Opposite the down-stage part of the window, and somewhat more than half-way down stage, is a sofa, big enough for three people. On it are sofa pillows. There is a curtain thrown over the back of the sofa, and another on the floor, to its Right. Directly above the sofa is a small table with a lamp. Directly below it a coffee table. To Left of this, about Center, a small ottoman. A little Up Left of this an arm chair, and just Up Left of this, a medium-sized drum table. Pictures, curtains, drapes, may be added to complete the scene.

NOTE FOR THE USE OF DIRECTORS PRODUCING THE PLAY. *A diagram of the stage will be found on p. 125. This shows the arrangement of the scene substantially as used in the professional production. However, it should be pointed out that certain details of the set itself and certain articles of furniture may be omitted and altered for purposes of simplification. For example, the hallway U.L. need not be quite so large as is indicated on the diagram, and possibly the front door might be in view of the audience. The large window to R. is scarcely used and may be easily omitted. While the stairs are necessary for a good deal of stage business, and the platform is most effective, a little ingenuity in arranging business might provide an easy substitute for the business now indicated as*

*taking place on the landing. The L. wall of the set might be
somewhat straighter than indicated on the diagram. The con-
sole-radio D.R. is not used. That was used in the original production simply as "dressing" and may be omitted. The hall
table may also be omitted and a chair put in its place.*

At Rise LIZZIE, *the maid, known as* LIZ, *is on-stage, holding a
flower-pot. After a second the front door slams, off U.R., and*
AGNES *appears U.R. in hallway. She has been shopping and carries packages and a newspaper. Packages are two stocking
boxes, which are never unwrapped, and a bag or larger pack-
age, in which are a small unglazed pot or pitcher, and a round
can of smoking tobacco. The moment the door slams* LIZ *turns
up to see who is entering.*

AGNES. (*As she enters*) Hiya, Liz. (LIZ *puts flower pot on table
above sofa*)

LIZ. Hello, Mrs. Carol.

AGNES. (*Crossing down to table behind sofa. Puts packages on
it*) Curtains look nice. (*Crosses L. to chair R. of sideboard.
Drops purse and gloves on chair.*)

LIZ. I think so. How was shopping? (*Folds curtain on back of
sofa. Puts it back on sofa*)

AGNES. (*Crossing L. to D.L. corner*) Not bad—I only got one
small dent on the right front fender.

LIZ. Your fault?

AGNES. Of course not. Men drivers!

LIZ. Did you call a cop?

AGNES. I didn't have to. It was a police car.

LIZ. Who was it?

AGNES. (*Putting can of tobacco on shelf D.L. corner*) Murray Beck and Al Rocco. I told them. I said, "If you'd been cruising around the way you're supposed to instead of parking, I wouldn't have hit you." (*Crosses R. to above sofa*)

LIZ. You were right, but don't tell me what they said!

AGNES. I hate men who laugh at logic. It's so anti-feminist.

LIZ. (*Picks up curtain from floor R. of sofa, folds it*) Get all your shopping done?

AGNES. (*Crossing down to sofa. Sits*) Well, I got the tobacco for Howard, and the paint for my ceramics, but then I lost the list, so I just took pot luck. (*Holding up newspaper*) Did you see what Barney White put in the paper today?

LIZ. (*Leaning over R. side of sofa to see*) She takes a nice picture. What does it say?

AGNES. It says, "Joan Carol, daughter of Mr. and Mrs. Howard G. Carol, who has been chosen to play the title role in this year's high school production of Victoria Regina. (*Liz crosses L. to up L. of sofa*) The cast will meet today for the first time to read the play under the watchful eye of Mr. Guy Thompson, well-known New York actor."

LIZ. You mean the school got a New York actor to come out here and put on the play?

AGNES. Yes. The English teacher coaches the football team and both practices fall at the same time.

LIZ. Oh, by the way, did Mr. Carol make another speech today?

AGNES. Yes, at the high school for the children. Why?

LIZ. Barney White called and said, "Ask Mr. Carol if I can quote him on his speech."

AGNES. Oh, dear.

LIZ. Well, don't worry yet. It may not be one of his major speeches.

AGNES. Let's hope not.

LIZ. I don't understand why people keep asking him to speak.

AGNES. (*Rises, crosses D.L. with box of paint and newspaper*) Well, Howard looks perfectly rational, and he is normally, but when he gets on a platform and looks down at that vast sea of faces, something happens to him.

LIZ. (*Crossing down L. to above drum table*) Have you ever been able to figure out what?

AGNES. It's mixed up with a lot of things. Howard's worked very happily at the bank for a number of years. He leaves here every morning with his brief-case, comes home every night with his brief-case and a bag of jelly beans for me. . . . (*Sits D.L. bench*) But he has never had a creative outlet.

LIZ. Having three daughters is pretty creative.

AGNES. Yes, but he's a man, and I guess every man wants a son.

LIZ. (*Crossing R. to table behind sofa to pick up flowers*) Would you like some coffee?

AGNES. Love some. (*Front door slams, and Howard Carol enters. He carries brief-case and hat in one hand. Wears coat*)

HOWARD. Hello everybody. (*Crosses down L. to drum table. Puts brief-case on it. AGNES rises, crosses R. to Howard*)

LIZ. Hello, Mr. Carol.

AGNES. (*Crossing R., carrying newspaper*) Hello, dear. Have you seen this? (*Hands* HOWARD *newspaper*)

HOWARD. Yeah, cute. Saw it at the office. (*Starts to put coat over back of armchair*) I was just going to hang it up, Liz. (*Crosses up to closet, hangs coat*)

LIZ. (*Crossing up, carrying flowers. Turns to Howard*) You'd better, if you want some coffee.

HOWARD. That's a very good basis for mutual understanding.

˜IZ. (*Crossing down L. to above drum table*) He seems happy.

AGNES. Yes, that's sometimes a bad sign. (HOWARD *re-enters from closet.* AGNES *crosses up R. to C.*) How did the speech go, dear? (LIZ *crosses L. to ceramic table L. Gets cardboard box*)

HOWARD. The kids seemed to love it. (*Crosses L. to drum table*)

LIZ. What was the speech about, Mr. Carol?

HOWARD. Manners, Liz.

LIZ. I'll get the coffee. (LIZ *exits into kitchen L.* HOWARD *reaches into his brief-case, takes from it a bag of jelly beans*)

HOWARD. (*Crossing R. to Agnes with jelly beans*) For you, lady.

AGNES. Thank you. (*Takes bag.* HOWARD *and* AGNES *embrace*)

HOWARD. You know I had to go to four places to get those today, and they don't make jelly beans the way they used to, either.

AGNES. Why do you suppose that is?

HOWARD. It's a lost art. There are no craftsmen left who hand roll them the way they used to. And have you noticed, black ones seem to be disappearing like buffalo.

AGNES. It's kind of sad to see the world change like this, isn't it?

HOWARD. It certainly is. (HOWARD *kisses Agnes*)

AGNES. Darling, are you sure you spoke about manners?

HOWARD. (*Crossing L. to above drum table*) Of course.

AGNES. What did you say?

HOWARD. Would you like to hear the speech?

AGNES. No, no. I don't want to hear the whole speech, just a brief résumé.

HOWARD. I said that most boys today are crude, unkempt, aggressive little monsters who have no respect for the opposite sex.

AGNES. Howard!

HOWARD. (*Crossing D.L. to small table. Puts brief-case on it.* AGNES *sits on R. arm of arm chair*) Well, it's the truth. But I don't blame this on the boys.

AGNES. You don't?

HOWARD. No, the girls are just as bad. They compete with the boys on every level. They race around, slapping them on the back, shouting at them on the street. No wonder the boys have no manners.

AGNES. Then the fault is with the girls?

HOWARD. No, the fault is with the parents; with the whole coeducational system that breeds this competition between boys and girls.

AGNES. Oh, now I see where this is leading. (*Rises*) Girls are forced to compete and take exercise forty-five minutes twice a week and boys come to regard them as physical equals.

HOWARD. Well, that's part of it.

AGNES. Then you mean you don't think girls should be forced to take exercise?

HOWARD. I mean I don't think any of those kids should be forced to do anything that infringes on their dignity as human beings. They should be allowed the freedom of being themselves, of making their own decisions.

AGNES. Well, this smacks of progressive parenthood!

HOWARD. I've always thought of myself as a free-thinker as far as our kids are concerned.

AGNES. I know, I've got the scars to prove it. (HOWARD *pats Agnes' back.* AGNES *crosses up to chair R. of sideboard, takes off her jacket, puts it and jelly beans down*) But, Howard, isn't there a contradiction here somewhere?

HOWARD. What do you mean? (*Crosses L. to table, takes papers from brief-case*)

AGNES. On the one hand you complain about the lack of manners in young people and on the other you say, "If they don't want manners, they shouldn't be forced to have them. Let them run wild."

HOWARD. (*Crossing R. to* AGNES) No, no, no. If those kids weren't so beset by restrictions and taboos they wouldn't feel the need to break loose and run wild later on.

AGNES. How do you account for your youngest child?

HOWARD. Virginia?

AGNES. Yes.

HOWARD. There is no accounting for her. She's the exception that proves the rule.

AGNES. Cliché, darling.

HOWARD. Well, maybe, but it's true. (*Crossing L. to above drum table*) I don't know why she is such a roughneck.

AGNES. Maybe if you showed as much interest in her as you do in Joan and Jeannie, you'd find out why.

HOWARD. I spend as much time on her as I do on the other two girls.

AGNES. (*Crossing L. to* HOWARD) But not with the same attitude, Howard. You've never treated Virginia the way you did the two older kids.

HOWARD. (*Crosses down L. around table to arm-chair, sits*) Oh, darling, let's not get off on that again.

AGNES. Well, if you don't practice what you preach, do you think it's wise to launch your theories from a public platform to a group of impressionable youngsters?

HOWARD. Listen. Those kids are perceptive and very mature. They knew exactly what I was trying to say, even if you don't. (AGNES *looks at* HOWARD, *shrugs*)

JOAN. (*Off*) Mom. . . . Mom! (*Front door slams*)

AGNES. Yes, dear. Trouble?

JOAN. (*Enters front door U.R.*) Mom, it's terrible.

HOWARD. Hya, beautiful.

JOAN. (*Running down L. to* HOWARD. *Kisses him*) Hello, Dad.

HOWARD. What's the matter?

JOAN. (*Crossing R. to sofa, puts her coat over L. back of sofa*) I'm so mad I could die! (LIZ *enters from kitchen, carrying coffee service, small cream pitcher, 2 cups and saucers. She crosses R. above armchair to coffee table and puts tray down on it*)

AGNES. About what? (*Sits on sofa*)

JOAN. She's an ugly old hag.

LIZ. Who is? (*Crosses up to R. of sofa*)

JOAN. *Victoria Regina.* We just read the play. I won't do it, I won't, I won't!

LIZ. Hang up your coat.

JOAN. I'll do it in a minute.

LIZ. Right now.

JOAN. I'm going out again in a little while.

AGNES. Right now.

JOAN. But, gee, Mom.

HOWARD. Right now. (JOAN *turns to look at* HOWARD)

JOAN. Parents! (*Picks up coat. Crosses up to closet, hangs coat.* (AGNES *pours cup of coffee*)

LIZ. (*Crossing L.*) Want a coke?

JOAN. Please Liz, I need one. (LIZ, *crossing L. to kitchen, takes one final look back at* AGNES *before she exits into kitchen*) I don't see why Helen Hayes would take an old part like that. (*Crosses down to C.*)

AGNES. (*Rises. Crossing L. to* HOWARD *with cup of coffee*) And mislead you.

JOAN. She keeps getting older in every scene. Do I have to do it?

AGNES. (*Crossing R. to* JOAN) Did you say you would? (*Crosses R. to sofa, sits. Pours herself cup of coffee*)

JOAN. But there are girls at school so much better equipped to play old women. (LIZ *enters from kitchen with a bottle of coke. Crosses R. to* JOAN, *takes* JOAN's *L. hand and puts bottle in it.* LIZ *crosses to kitchen, exits*)

AGNES. If you gave your word, there is only one honest course for you to follow. (LIZ, *crossing L. to kitchen, nods approval*)

JOAN. But I only took the part so I could get out of gym twice a week.

HOWARD. Huh? I don't quite follow that.

JOAN. (*Turns L. to* HOWARD) Practice for the play and gym periods come at the same time every week.

HOWARD. And all this time I thought you were seeking culture.

JOAN. (*Crossing L. to* HOWARD) So in view of that I don't think I should be forced to do Victoria, do you, Dad?

HOWARD. Unless you or this Mr. Thompson can find someone to

take over the part before practice starts, you most certainly have to do what you promised. Right, dear?

AGNES. Right.

JOAN. (*Crossing R. to sofa. Sits on L. arm*) Well. (*Front door slams*) I don't understand that reasoning.

HOWARD. I'm sorry. (JEANNIE *enters front door, carrying school-books*)

JEANNIE. Hello, everybody. (*Puts books on hall table, crosses down fast to* HOWARD *in armchair, puts her arm around his neck. She carries folded sheet of paper*)

HOWARD. Hello, kitten.

JEANNIE. Hello, Daddy. Your speech today was simply wonderful.

HOWARD. I'm glad you liked it.

JEANNIE. All the girls at school say you must be the most terrific man in the world.

JOAN. Everybody adores you. They say they wish all their fathers were as liberal-minded as you are.

HOWARD. Well, it's just a question of saying the right thing at the right time.

JEANNIE. But it was such a courageous stand to take.

HOWARD. Oh, not really.

JEANNIE. (*Crosses R. to C.*) Well, we want you to know that every girl in the junior and senior classes support your stand and was moved to action by your stirring words.

HOWARD. You see, dear?

JEANNIE. (*Crossing R. above sofa*) Will you sign this, Mother?

AGNES. What is it?

JEANNIE. (*Hands sheet of paper to* AGNES.) A petition.

JOAN. (*Turns to* JEANNIE) How many signatures have we got?

JEANNIE. Over a hundred. (*Crosses L. to C.*) And, Daddy, we want you to know, we'll back you against any and all opposition, regardless of the consequences.

AGNES. Howard, have you seen this?

HOWARD. What?

AGNES. (*Rises, crosses L. to C. and reads*) "We the undersigned do herewith subscribe to the statement of Howard G. Carol—quote—'I would abolish gymnasium for girls because it infringes on their rights as individuals, and no one should be forced to do anything he doesn't want to do'." Unquote. (*Unrolls paper, hands it to* HOWARD. *Crosses L. to L. of armchair*)

HOWARD. Who put out this petition?

JEANNIE. The girls of the junior and senior classes.

HOWARD. But, kitten, you had no right to circulate a petition without asking me.

JOAN. We only quoted you. (*Crosses up to sideboard, puts coke bottle on it*)

JEANNIE. (*Crossing L. to armchair*) And you don't mind, do you?

HOWARD. Well, I didn't mean to make an issue out of it.

AGNES. Howard, you'd better do something to stop this.

JOAN. You mean you said it and didn't mean it? (*Crosses down to R. of* HOWARD)

HOWARD. Well, I didn't mean to abolish gym for girls.

JEANNIE. Daddy!

JOAN. Daddy!

HOWARD. Basically it was a speech on manners.

JOAN. You mean you approve of gym for girls?

HOWARD. Well, not exactly.

AGNES. Howard, what did you say?

HOWARD. (*Hands petition to* JOAN *and takes speech from his R. breast pocket and reads.* JOAN *folds up petition and hands it to* JEANNIE, *who puts it on table*) I said, "perhaps one reason that young men do not conform to the rules of etiquette is that they see girls playing volley ball and basketball, thus losing sight of their femininity."

JOAN. (*Crossing down R. to D.R. of ottoman*) And then you said it.

HOWARD. Yeah. Huh? Well, extemporaneously I may have said that perhaps one idea might be to change the method of gym for girls.

AGNES. What sort of change, dear?

HOWARD. Instead of those rough sports let them take long walks during those periods.

JEANNIE. I agree with you, Daddy.

JOAN. So do I. (*Sits on ottoman*)

HOWARD. It stands to reason, Agnes, that competitive sports are too violent for young girls. (*Looks at* JOAN)

AGNES. (*Crossing R. to coffee table*) I'll bet the school board is looking for the highest tree in town right now. (*Sits on sofa*)

JEANNIE. I think Daddy absolutely put his finger on the root of the problem. (*Front door slams*)

JOAN. I think your speech was positively breath-taking. (GINGER *enters front door, carrying school books*)

GINGER. (*Looking off R.*) I think all men stink. (*Crosses down to sofa. Drops books on table behind sofa, drops coat over L. back of sofa*) Hello, Pop.

HOWARD. Don't retract that remark just because I'm here.

GINGER. I wasn't going to.

AGNES. What's wrong between you and Tommy today?

GINGER. He always wants me to do something I don't want to do, because he doesn't want me to do something he doesn't want me to do. That's the trouble with men.

AGNES. Now you know that's true, Howard.

HOWARD. Yeah, it's confused enough to be.

JEANNIE. (*Crosses L. one step*) What does Tommy want you to do?

GINGER. (*Crosses L. to C.*) Be a cheer leader.

HOWARD. What's wrong with that?

GINGER. Nothing, if you want to be a cheer leader. I just don't want to be a cheer leader.

AGNES. Then don't do it, darling. Don't let anyone infringe on your basic right.

GINGER. I won't.

JOAN. (*Turns to* GINGER) Why don't you put a washer on that drip?

GINGER (*Crosses L. a step*) He's not a drip. He just frightens you because he's got brains.

JOAN. (*Turns R. on ottoman*) He doesn't frighten Eddie, though, does he?

GINGER. Oh, your big four-letter man—b-o-r-e.

HOWARD. All right, that's enough. (GINGER *smirks at* JOAN, *who turns front*)

GINGER. (*Crossing R. to sofa*) Where's Lizzie, Mom?

AGNES. Try the kitchen.

GINGER. (*Crosses L. to U.R. of ottoman*) Ask Eddie what happened yesterday. (JOAN *turns to* GINGER. GINGER *crosses L. to kitchen, exits*)

JOAN. Gee, she gripes me. (JEANNIE *looks at* HOWARD, *shrugs*)

AGNES. Why? (JEANNIE *crosses to D.L. corner, and sits on bench. She takes small jar from ceramic table, looks at it*)

JOAN. (*Rises, crossing R. to L. of sofa*) She has no dignity. She runs around the halls at school like a wild gazelle. (*Crosses L. to C. To* HOWARD) Yesterday during lunch hour she was wrestling with two boys—sophomores.

HOWARD. She's just high spirited, that's all.

JOAN. Everybody laughs at her, and it reflects on my standing among the seniors.

AGNES. That means you live in reflected laughter. I should think that would be a very happy situation.

JOAN. (*Crossing R. to sofa*) I can see you don't understand, Mom.

AGNES. Take it up with your father. He's very understanding.

JOAN. (*Turns L., crosses to* HOWARD) Daddy, do I have to do Victoria?

HOWARD. How did we get back to that?

JOAN. (*Sits on ottoman*) I have to circulate petitions and I won't have time now that you've endorsed your stand.

JEANNIE. Don't you want to do it?

JOAN. No.

JEANNIE. Do you think maybe I could do it?

JOAN. (*Rises, runs L. to* JEANNIE *upstage of armchair*) Oh, you'd be much better than I would and you'd save my life.

JEANNIE. All right, I'll try. Let's go upstairs and read a couple of scenes. (JOAN *and* JEANNIE *cross R. to stairs*)

JOAN. (*Crossing R. to table, behind sofa. Picks up books*) Good.

Then we'll tell Mr. Thompson about it tomorrow before classes.

JEANNIE. (JOAN *and* JEANNIE *begin to climb stairs*) He's going to be down at the drug store later. Let's tell him then.

JOAN. All right.

AGNES. Just a minute, girls. (JOAN *and* JEANNIE *stop.* AGNES *rises, crosses up to R. of bottom of stairs*) It seems to me you're both riding roughshod over a moral issue.

JOAN. What do you mean, Mother?

AGNES. Joan, Mr. Thompson chose you and you have no right to pass the part on to your sister or anybody else without his knowledge and consent.

JOAN. (*Crosses down stairs to* AGNES) Even if I don't want to do it, and Jeannie does?

AGNES. That decision is not for you and Jeannie to settle between you.

JOAN. (*Crosses down to U.R. of ottoman.* JEANNIE *crosses down stairs*) But Daddy said nobody should be forced—

AGNES. Howard. . . .

HOWARD. I know what I said, but that has nothing to do with this.

JOAN. You mean you were wrong?

HOWARD. No, but you can't apply one rule to every issue.

JEANNIE. (*Crossing down to L. of* HOWARD) Not even if they're related issues?

HOWARD. Sometimes, kitten, but not this time.

JOAN. Why not, Daddy?

HOWARD. Well, because, darling, you gave your word before I made the speech. (AGNES *crosses down to behind L. end of sofa*)

JEANNIE. But I want the part and I don't want to take gym.

JOAN. So doesn't that make everything all right?

HOWARD. Agnes. . . .

AGNES. (*Sits on L. back of sofa*) Don't drag me into this.

JOAN. If I ask Mr. Thompson and he says yes, is it all right then, Daddy?

HOWARD. Oh, all right, ask him. But be sure you don't force him.

JOAN. Oh, Daddy, we won't.

JEANNIE. Thank you, Daddy.

JOAN. You're wonderful. (JOAN *and* JEANNIE *kiss* HOWARD. JEANNIE *musses* HOWARD's *hair. Girls run up to foot of stairs*) Oh, call me when Eddie comes, will you, Mom? (JOAN *and* JEANNIE *exit upstairs, giggling*)

AGNES. All right. Well, dear, you're certainly developing a great sense of organized chaos.

HOWARD. It's just that social relationships are a little difficult at times.

AGNES. (*Crosses L. Sits on ottoman*) You know, Howard, there are times when everybody does things they don't want to do.

HOWARD. Did you get a dent on the right front fender of my car today?

AGNES. (*Rises*) Yes.

HOWARD. How?

AGNES. Doing something I didn't want to do. (*Crossing L. above armchair to D.L. corner*) I ran into a police car. (HOWARD *groans*) Oh, Barney White's been calling you. (*Sits on bench D.L.*)

HOWARD. What did he want?

AGNES. It seems he wants to quote you on your speech.

HOWARD. Oh. . . . (*Rises, crosses up to phone on phone table U.*)

AGNES. He'll probably want a picture, too.

HOWARD. I haven't got a picture. (*Dials number*)

AGNES. Maybe you ought to have some made?

HOWARD. Maybe I should. You get so upset over these things. (*Into phone*) Hello, Barn. . . . Howie . . . did you call me? . . . well, it was nothing.

AGNES. Oh, come now.

HOWARD. (*Into phone*) Well, the kids sort of amplified it. . . . You what? . . . Where'd you get ahold of a copy of the petition? . . . They did, huh? (*Looks upstairs. Sits in chair R. of phone table*) Well, I suggested that they go for long walks during those periods. You know what George Washington said, "Long walks are the best exercise."

AGNES. He must have said something else.

HOWARD. (*Into phone*) Sure, Barney, go ahead and print it. Can't do any harm. (*Rises*) Thanks for calling. (*Hangs up*) Seems to have created quite a stir. (*Crosses down to above drum table. Picks up petition, reads it*)

AGNES. Uh-huh.

HOWARD. (*Crosses L. to* AGNES) You don't understand this, darling, because you're not as close to the problems of the young people as I am.

AGNES. No. I'm in the house all day. (*Front door bell rings*) I'll get it, Liz. (*Rises, crosses U.R., stopping behind* HOWARD) You know, Howard, this kind of reasoning can lead to a terrible disease called "Hoof-in-the-mouth." (*Crosses U.R. to front door*)

HOWARD. (*Following* AGNES) Even boys aren't as aggressive and overt as some girls today. (*Looks up stairs*)

AGNES. (*Off U.R.*) Now really, Howard.

EDDIE. (*Off U.R.*) Hya, Mrs. Carol. (HOWARD *winces, crosses down to armchair*)

AGNES. (*Off. Mimicking* EDDIE) Hya, Eddie. . . . Come in. (EDDIE *enters from front door, followed by* AGNES)

EDDIE. Hya, Mr. Carol.

HOWARD. Hello, Eddie. Sit down. (*Sits in armchair*)

EDDIE. Thanks. (*Sits on sofa*)

AGNES. (*Calling upstairs*) Joan, Eddie is here.

JOAN. (*Off, upstairs*) I'll be down in a minute, Mother.

AGNES. (*Imitating* JOAN) All right. *Crosses down to C.* HOWARD *puts petition on drum table*)

EDDIE. (*Sprawled comfortably on sofa*) What do you think of a guy coming all the way from New York to try and steal my girl?

AGNES. (*Stops R. of* HOWARD) I beg your pardon?

EDDIE. This actor. That's why he gave my girl the part in the play. But he better not fool around with my girl. (*Settles back on sofa*) I guess he doesn't realize I'm the big man in this school. (HOWARD *picks up Time magazine from drum table, looks into it*)

AGNES. (*Looks at* HOWARD) I guess not. (*Crosses to D.L. corner below armchair. Sits on bench, begins working on her ceramic.* EDDIE *sits up on sofa, crosses and recrosses his legs*)

EDDIE. (*Rises*) Hey, Mr. Carol, that was some speech you made in school today.

HOWARD. (*Smiles at* EDDIE, *looks at* AGNES) Thanks, Eddie.

EDDIE. (*Crosses to C.*) After school all the guys were bowing to the girls— (*Bows*) and holding their coats. (*To* AGNES) It was a regular eighteenth century ball.

AGNES. I'll bet.

EDDIE. (*Crossing L. above armchair to* AGNES) I got so swept away I opened the car door for Joan. (*To* HOWARD) I never did that before in my life. (*To* AGNES) She was so shocked she staggered.

HOWARD. She's just not accustomed to gentility. (*Reads magazine.* EDDIE *does a take*)

EDDIE. Oh. (EDDIE *looks from* HOWARD, *who is reading, to* AGNES, *who is painting. Folds arms and brushes his hair. Then he runs up R. to foot of stairs, looks up. Crosses down C. to U.L. of sofa, and bursts into several hot licks of music—humming bits of jazz—at the end of which, he falls on his back on sofa.* HOWARD *takes a drink of his coffee, his hand shaking nervously.* EDDIE *sits up)*

EDDIE. That always makes my father nervous.

HOWARD. Yeah. How's your father's ulcer, Eddie?

EDDIE. (*Rises. Crosses L. to ottoman, puts L. foot on it*) Mr. Carol, I knew there was something I had to tell you.

HOWARD. What is it?

EDDIE. Football practice starts tomorrow.

HOWARD. (*To* AGNES) Did you hear that, dear?

AGNES. No, I'm tuned out.

EDDIE. (*Takes foot off ottoman*) Sure does. So get your tickets early or you'll never see me run.

HOWARD. How's the team going to be this year?

EDDIE. Well, as I said to the coach this afternoon, I said, "Just put ten other kids on the field and give me the ball."

AGNES. That was nice of you.

EDDIE. (*Looks at* AGNES) I'm murder on a field.

AGNES. I think you're murder off.

EDDIE. Thanks. (HOWARD *looks at* EDDIE. EDDIE *looks at* AGNES. HOWARD *looks away, amused*) Did I tell you how many colleges are trying to get me?

HOWARD. Not yet.

EDDIE. (*Starts L. to* HOWARD) I got the list right here. (GINGER *and* LIZ *enter from kitchen.* GINGER *crosses to U.R. of ottoman,* LIZ *crosses to U.L. of drum table*)

GINGER. Hya, muscle-head.

AGNES. Virginia.

EDDIE. Hya, kid. (*Breaks R., crosses to sofa*)

GINGER. What are you doing, showing Mom and Pop your scrap book?

EDDIE. Why don't you stop? (*Sits on sofa*)

LIZ. Tell them what happened yesterday.

GINGER. No. It will embarrass him.

EDDIE. It was an accident.

GINGER. It was not.

HOWARD. What happened?

GINGER. He insulted me.

EDDIE. I did not.

GINGER. You did so, you reactionary.

HOWARD. Never mind that. What happened?

GINGER. (*Turns back to* HOWARD) He called Tommy Green a sissy.

HOWARD. I don't see how that concerns you.

LIZ. (*Crossing D.R. to L. of drum table*) Let her finish.

HOWARD. Finish.

GINGER. Every time one boy wants to insult another, he calls him a sissy. And by that they imply that girls are inferior to boys.

LIZ. And they're not.

AGNES. I see your point.

HOWARD. Pass.

GINGER. So yesterday after school, when the track team was out I challenged him to a hundred yard dash.

EDDIE. I didn't want to race a girl.

GINGER. At first he just laughed, but after I needled him for a while, he said he'd show me.

HOWARD. Well, what happened?

GINGER. (*Looking at* EDDIE) I ran him into the ground.

AGNES. You mean you beat him?

GINGER. By five yards.

EDDIE. Three yards. (HOWARD *laughs.* GINGER *crosses down to* HOWARD)

AGNES. Howard.

HOWARD. That's the funniest thing I ever heard.

EDDIE. I had a bad foot. (JOAN *and* JEANNIE *come down stairs.* JOAN *descends to floor level,* JEANNIE *stays a step or two above her*)

GINGER. You did not.

JOAN. I'm ready, Eddie.

EDDIE. (*Rises, crosses up to arch, limping*) Come on, let's go.

JOAN. (*Stops* EDDIE) Eddie, what's wrong with your foot?

EDDIE. I sprained it.

JOAN. When?

EDDIE. Yesterday.

JOAN. But you weren't limping this afternoon.

EDDIE. Come on, it's late. (*Exits to front door*)

JEANNIE. (*Cossing down stairs and down L. to* HOWARD) Bye, Daddy. (*Kisses* HOWARD. JOAN *takes her coat from closet, puts it on*)

HOWARD. Bye, darling, and Joanie, you get back here in time for dinner.

JOAN. All right.

HOWARD. Cause if you don't I'll send Virginia out to run you and your athlete down. (HOWARD, JEANNIE, GINGER, LIZ *and* AGNES *laugh*)

JOAN. Daddy. (*Exits to front door*)

JEANNIE. (*Crossing up to closet, blows* HOWARD *a kiss*) Bye (*Gets coat from closet, exits to front door.* HOWARD, AGNES *and* GINGER *ad lib goodbyes*)

HOWARD. (*Looks at* GINGER, *stops laughing*) As for you, Miss . . .

GINGER. What?

HOWARD. Don't ever do a thing like that again.

GINGER. Why not?

HOWARD. It's unladylike.

GINGER. But, Pop, I *can* beat him.

HOWARD. Never mind that. From now on try to remember you're a girl.

GINGER. (*Crossing L. to above drum table*) I wish I were a man.

LIZ. (*Crosses D.R. a step*) Would you rather have him live with the delusion girls are inferior and be disillusioned later in life? (GINGER *picks up Ms of* HOWARD'S *speech from drum table*)

HOWARD. I don't care anything about him, Elizabeth. I'm talking about her.

GINGER. Is this a copy of your speech?

HOWARD. Yes, it is.

GINGER. May I read it?

HOWARD. Sure, if you want to.

GINGER. Thanks. (*Takes Ms, crosses R. to U.R. of armchair. Stops*) Pop?

HOWARD. Huh?

GINGER. Do you love me?

HOWARD. Of course I love you.

GINGER. I'm glad, cause you're really going to have to. (*Runs up and exits upstairs.* LIZ *crosses R. to sofa, gets* GINGER's *coat, crosses up to closet, hangs up coat. Then crosses down C.*)

HOWARD. What do you suppose that means?

AGNES. I don't know, but they're going to have to take Virginia for very long walks.

HOWARD. Oh, Lizzie. . . .

LIZ. (*Stops U.R. of armchair*) Yeah?

HOWARD. This is mere curiosity, but didn't I just see you hang up Virginia's coat?

LIZ. Yes, you did. Why?

HOWARD. I don't mean to offend you, but I just wondered. Her above all?

AGNES. "She," dear.

HOWARD. "She"—doesn't sound right. She above all?

LIZ. Why shouldn't I hang up her coat?

HOWARD. I just don't want you to spoil her.

AGNES. Nobody is spoiling her, Howard.

LIZ. You spoiled the other two.

HOWARD. That's silly.

LIZ. It's not silly.

AGNES. She's right.

HOWARD. How?

LIZ. They kiss you and bully you into doing anything they like.

AGNES. But the minute Virginia tries to do something, then you become the father.

LIZ. And I don't see why she should be handicapped just because she wasn't a boy.

AGNES. That's why she hung up her coat.

LIZ. So there.

HOWARD. (*Waves his hand in despair*) I never seem to win one of these things. (LIZ *crosses U.L. to sideboard, and sets something—doily—straight*) What is it, my choice of words or lack of phrasing, or what? Elizabeth—(LIZ *crosses down to U.L. of drum table*)—from here on out, she has my consent to run against five horses at Hialeah Park every day.

LIZ. She'd win. (*Front door bell.* LIZ *crosses R. to front door*)

HOWARD. (*To* AGNES) If you'd listen to me we wouldn't have had all this trouble about gym for girls and running foot races.

AGNES. What do you mean?

HOWARD. I told you three times, have a son, but no, you wouldn't listen. (*Front door slams.* LIZ *and* TOMMY GREEN *enter*)

LIZ. (*Crossing L. to foot of stairs*) It's Tommy Green.

HOWARD. Hello, Tommy. Come in.

AGNES. Hello, Tommy.

TOMMY. (*Crossing down to C.*) Hello, Mrs. Carol . . . Mr. Carol.

LIZ. (*Crossing upstairs a few steps*) Ginger. . . .

GINGER. (*Off*) Will you come up for a minute, Liz?

LIZ. Tommy's here.

GINGER. (*Off*) Tell him to wait.

LIZ. (*To* TOMMY) Wait. (*Exits upstairs*)

TOMMY. Yes, ma'am.

HOWARD. Sit down, Tommy.

TOMMY. Thank you, sir. (*Crosses down to L. end of sofa, sits*) I heard your speech today, Mr. Carol.

AGNES. Everybody did.

TOMMY. And I must say it was quite fascinating.

HOWARD. Thanks, Tommy. I understand football practice starts tomorrow.

TOMMY. Yes, sir.—There are a few points in that speech I'd like to discuss with you.

HOWARD. You don't play football, do you, Tommy?

TOMMY. No, sir. Mr. Carol, you said . . .

HOWARD. I wish I were back in school. I'd run that Eddie Davis ragged. Did I ever tell you about my football days?

TOMMY. Not recently.

HOWARD. Oh. (LIZ *enters down stairs, followed by* GINGER, *who carries a small book.* LIZ *crosses L. to sideboard, picks up coke bottle, and exits into kitchen*)

GINGER. Hya, Tommy. (TOMMY *rises, crosses up to* GINGER, *below foot of stairs*)

TOMMY. Hya, Ginger.

GINGER. What do you want?

TOMMY. Well, I thought maybe you'd like to walk down to the drug store and take a look at the New York actor.

GINGER. (*Indicating her book*) No, thanks. I'm doing some research on individual rights.

TOMMY. Oh. Well, there's something I want to tell you.

GINGER. Well, tell me.

TOMMY. You don't have to be a cheer leader if you don't want to.

GINGER. Thanks.

TOMMY. I believe everyone should be allowed to do what he wants to do.

HOWARD. Hey, hey, hey! Just a minute, young man.

TOMMY. (*Turns L. to* HOWARD) Yes, sir?

HOWARD. (*Rises, crossing U. to L. of* GINGER) Are you the one responsible for teaching this human dynamo she's the equal of anyone, anywhere?

GINGER. No one had to teach me that.

HOWARD. I wasn't talking to you, Flash.

GINGER. Go ahead, Tommy. Tell him what you believe.

TOMMY. Well sir, in principle I believe anyone should be allowed to compete on any level they choose.

HOWARD. I see. . . .

TOMMY. (GINGER *looks at* TOMMY *admiringly*) To deprive any person, man or woman, of his constitutional rights is to infringe upon the fundamental law of the land and deny them their basic freedom as set down by our founding fathers, when they said, "We hold these truths to be self-evident; that all men are created equal. . . ."

HOWARD. Well, thanks, Tommy. (*Crosses down to R. of armchair.* TOMMY *follows* HOWARD. GINGER *moves down R., sits on L. arm of sofa*)

TOMMY. In other words, it is the privilege and the responsibility of every American to think the way he likes, act the way he likes, talk the way he likes, vote the way he likes, and to worship as he pleases.

HOWARD. That's very true, but . . . (*Crosses down,* TOMMY *following*)

TOMMY. And I would like to say, regardless of race, color, creed or sex, there are no second-class citizens of these United States, and we, as liberty-loving people, must seek out the evil, never retreat from the heat of battle, and destroy the forces of reaction that impede progress. (HOWARD *turns back to see if more speech is coming*) That speech got me last year's debating medal. (GINGER *rises, crosses R., sits in C. of sofa*)

HOWARD. I can see why. (*Crosses L. to D.L. corner, sits on bench*)

TOMMY. (*Crossing L. to above armchair*) I wrote it myself.

AGNES. Tommy . . .

TOMMY. Yes, ma'am?

AGNES. You prefaced all that by saying, "in principle, I believe
. . . " but the point is how do you feel about Virginia running
foot races against Eddie?

TOMMY. Mrs. Carol, I don't feel she should do it.

GINGER. What?

TOMMY. I can't help it. That's the way I feel.

GINGER. Then you don't believe what you've always said.

TOMMY. (*Crossing R. to C.*) Yes I do.

GINGER. But you mean I shouldn't compete against Eddie?

TOMMY. (*Crossing R. to sofa*) Sure you should with Eddie, or
with any other man. (*Sits on L. of sofa*) But you should compete
as a girl, not a boy.

GINGER. If everybody is equal what difference does it make how
I compete?

TOMMY. It makes a difference because men and women are
equal, but not the same. (*Front*) If there weren't any difference I'd go out on dates with Eddie Davis.

GINGER. What for? I can run faster than he can.

TOMMY. Look, Ginger, that's not why I like you.

GINGER. Why do you like me?

TOMMY. Because you're a girl.

GINGER. And that's why you don't want me to compete against Eddie?

TOMMY. Yes.

GINGER. (*Rises, backs R. to R. end of sofa*) Then you don't think of me as an equal.

TOMMY. Sure I do, but I think of you as a girl first.

GINGER. Well, I want to be an equal first. (*Crosses U. and L. above sofa to U.L. of it*)

TOMMY. (*Rises, crosses U.L.*) Then go ahead, I don't want to talk about it anymore.

GINGER. (*Crossing L. to Tommy*) You don't want to talk about it because you know you're wrong.

TOMMY. (*Front*) I want to go home and think. Bye, Mrs. Carol . . . Sir. (TOMMY *crosses U.R. and exits front door*)

HOWARD and AGNES. Bye, Tommy.

GINGER. (*Following Tommy*) Wait a minute. You can't get out of it that easy. (*Exits front door*)

HOWARD. (*Rises, crosses R. above armchair*) Virginia seems to have discovered a new sex—boys, girls, and equals. (*Sits in armchair.* GINGER *re-enters front door*)

GINGER. (*Crossing down to U.L. of sofa*) I worry about that boy. (AGNES *rises*) He's terribly confused. (*Crosses down to sofa, sits on L. arm*)

AGNES. (*Crossing R. to U.C.*) Well, never mind, darling. One of you will straighten out.

GINGER. Pop, don't you think it's wonderful I can run faster than anyone else in the whole school?

HOWARD. No, I don't, Virginia. I agree with Tommy. You shouldn't be trying to run faster than anyone else. (AGNES *crosses R. to sofa and chucks Virginia under chin, then sits on sofa*)

GINGER. (*Looks at* AGNES, *then back to* HOWARD) Oh. Pop, did you really mean all the things you said in that speech today? (*Front door bell*)

HOWARD. If I didn't mean them I wouldn't have said them. (LIZ *enters from kitchen, crosses R. to front door*)

GINGER. You heard what he said, Mom. (*Rises, crosses L. to Howard, musses his hair. Crosses up to stairs, exits.* HOWARD *rises, crosses up to sideboard*)

HOWARD. That kid will be the death of me. (LIZ *enters from front door*)

LIZ. It's Mr. Wilson, the high school principal. (LIZ *crosses L., exits into kitchen.* AGNES *rises*)

HOWARD. Hello, Bob, come on in.

WILSON. (*Entering from front door*) Hello, Agnes . . . Howie. (WILSON *and* HOWARD *shake hands*)

HOWARD. Can I take your coat?

WILSON. I can only stay a minute. (*Drops hat on table behind sofa*)

HOWARD. How about a drink?

WILSON. Thanks, no.—Let's get right to the point, shall we?

HOWARD. Yeah, fine.

WILSON. (*Crossing L. two steps*) First, I would like you to do me a favor. If in some wild moment, I should ever ask you to speak again—please turn me down. (*Takes coat off, crosses R., drops coat over L. back of sofa.* AGNES *sits in C. of sofa*)

HOWARD. I will be delighted.

WILSON. Thank you. Now on that disagreeable note, let's go forward, shall we? (*Takes Ms petition from pocket*) Have you seen this petition? (*Unrolls petition a little*)

HOWARD. Yes, I have.

WILSON. Doesn't it make you shudder? (*Folds petition, puts it back in pocket*)

HOWARD. No, it doesn't. (*Crosses D.L. to L. of drum table*)

WILSON. Obviously you haven't heard about Virginia. (HOWARD *turns R.*) This afternoon she reported for the boys' football team.

AGNES. (*Rises*) Oh, no!

WILSON. Oh, yes.

HOWARD. (*Crossing R. to Wilson*) Football? Agnes, call her down here. (WILSON *crosses L. to above armchair*)

AGNES. (*Crosses up to foot of stairs. Calling*) Virginia.

HOWARD. (*Crossing R. to Wilson*) We'll settle this in five minutes.

GINGER (*Off*) Yes, Mom?

HOWARD. (*Crossing up to foot of stairs*) Come down here.

AGNES. But surely even if she insists on playing, there is no problem about stopping her.

WILSON. (*Leaning on back of armchair*) Unfortunately Agnes, there's no rule that says she can't play.

HOWARD. Well, you can declare girls ineligible.

AGNES. On what grounds? (WILSON *crosses down to L. of drum table*) I'm not defending her, Howard, I'm just asking.

HOWARD. Do me a favor and don't ask questions like that in front of her. (GINGER *enters down stairs*)

GINGER. Did you call me, Pop?

HOWARD. I certainly did. Sit down, Virginia.

GINGER. (*Crossing down to L. end of sofa*) Yes, sir. Hello, Mr. Wilson. (*Sits C. of sofa.* AGNES *crosses D.R. to R. end of sofa, stands*)

HOWARD. (*Crosses D. to L. of sofa*) Virginia, what is this foolishness about your playing football?

GINGER. You mustn't shout at children, Pop. You must reason with them.

AGNES. (*Sitting on sofa R. of Ginger*) Darling, what on earth made you do a thing like this?

GINGER. Pop's speech. I've always wanted to play football and he said, "Everybody should be allowed to do what they want to do."

HOWARD. No, no. No, I said, "Nobody should be forced to do what they don't want to do."

WILSON. What's the difference?

HOWARD. There is a great deal of difference.

GINGER. Well, I don't want to not play football.

HOWARD. Well, you're not going to.

GINGER. You're being arbitrary, Pop.

AGNES. But, darling, don't you realize it's a dangerous game? You might get hurt.

GINGER. I'd make a great half-back.

HOWARD. Virginia, what makes you think you can play football?

GINGER. (*Rises. To Howard*) I can run, I can kick. You were a great half-back, and there's no reason why I can't be just as good as you were.

AGNES. Look, Virginia. Your father. . . . (*Pulls Ginger down to sofa*)

HOWARD. Virginia, you're not going to play football, and that's final.

GINGER. You didn't object to Jeannie playing in *Victoria*.

HOWARD. That's different.

GINGER. It's not different.

WILSON. Young lady, you'll force me to pass a regulation forbidding girls to partake in any sport.

GINGER. (*Rises. Crossing L. to C.*) All right Mr. Wilson, go ahead. But if I'm denied my athletic rights I'll refuse to attend classes.

WILSON. Then I'll have you expelled.

GINGER. (*Crossing L. to above armchair*) Let me remind you, sir, the Constitution and the Bill of Rights guarantee every American citizen life, liberty and the pursuit of happiness.

WILSON. Are you going to let her talk to me like that?

HOWARD. What? No. (*Crossing L. to Ginger*) Virginia, surely you understand we're only thinking of you. (*Sits on back of armchair*)

GINGER. It's not really me you're thinking of, Pop. It's yourself.

HOWARD. What do you mean by that?

GINGER. You're afraid if I go out for the team people will laugh at you.

HOWARD. Why should they laugh at me?

WILSON. Because of that preposterous speech you made this afternoon. (HOWARD *rises*)

GINGER. You're putting your vanity above my freedom of choice.

HOWARD. I'm doing no such thing.

WILSON. Yes, you are.

HOWARD. Whose side are you on?

WILSON. My side. I think you're both wrong.

GINGER. Sure, because you're afraid this change will lead to a lot of other changes in school.

AGNES. Believe me, Virginia, that is not what I'm worried about. (HOWARD *turns R.*)

GINGER. (*Crossing R. below Howard to L. end of sofa*) Mom, you're being old-fashioned.

AGNES. I am?

GINGER. Yes. You've accepted the theory that women shouldn't compete with men. (*To Howard*) Well, *I* haven't.

HOWARD. (*Crossing R. to Ginger*) Virginia, if you persist in this nonsense, I'll cut off your allowance.

GINGER. I don't need any money, I'm in training. (WILSON *holds hand to his face*) You see, Pop, I don't ask to be on the team. All I ask is a chance to try out for it.

AGNES. (*Holding hand out to Ginger. Pulls her down to sofa*) But, darling, I don't think you're equipped to play football.

GINGER. (*Sits on sofa L. of Agnes*) You can't say that until you've given me a chance.

AGNES. But you're a girl.

GINGER. Lots of athletes are.

HOWARD. (*Kneels L. of Ginger*) They don't play football against men.

GINGER. Because men won't let them. You're supposed to be sports, and all the time you're afraid we'll be equal to you.

AGNES. Or better than you. (HOWARD *rises, crosses L. to R. of ottoman*)

HOWARD. Well, there seems to be only one solution.

WILSON. And what, may I ask, is that?

HOWARD. Go upstairs, Virginia, if you don't mind. We'll discuss this later.

GINGER. Yes, sir. Thanks, Mom. (*Kisses Agnes on cheek*)

AGNES. You're welcome, Virginia.

GINGER. (*Rises*) Good evening, Mr. Wilson. (*To Howard*) I'm going to bed tonight at eight o'clock, just like the coach ordered. (AGNES *rises.* GINGER *exits toward front door, and returns carrying pair of football pants stuffed with a jersey and shoulder guards in one hand, and a football helmet in other*)

HOWARD. (*Crossing up C.*) What have you got there? (AGNES *crosses up to stairs*)

GINGER. My football equipment. (*Exits up stairs, followed by* AGNES)

HOWARD. Virginia, you can't practice in the house.

WILSON. Well, what's your solution?

HOWARD. (*Crossing down to behind sofa*) I think some of the things she says make a great deal of sense.

WILSON. I might have expected you to say that.

HOWARD. What does the coach think?

WILSON. (*Crossing down to armchair*) We don't pay the coach to think. (*Sits in armchair*) We pay the coach to teach English.

HOWARD. (*Crossing down to sofa. Sits*) That's fine talk from an educator, Bob.

WILSON. Howie, you certainly don't believe what you said this afternoon.

HOWARD. Bob, don't you think that a child should be allowed to seek his own fulfillment?

WILSON. (*Rises. Crossing R. behind sofa to R. arm of sofa*) Not if it means complete chaos.

HOWARD. If chaos in your school is the result of the searching and probing of a fourteen year old, then your foundations are rotten.

WILSON. Now, wait a minute. (*Sits on R. end of sofa*) I would like to follow your reasoning through to its illogical conclusion. If she wanted to burn down the house, would you let her do it?

HOWARD. No. Of course not. I'd try to show her why it was wrong.

WILSON. Why?

HOWARD. Because if she burned down the house she'd have no place to live.

WILSON. Suppose she only wanted to burn out one room?

HOWARD. It would depend upon which room. If she felt she had to do it, I might just let her. And if she believes she can play football, I think she deserves a chance to try.

WILSON. You do?

HOWARD. I certainly do. I made a statement, and by gosh, I'll stick to it.

WILSON. You don't think that's wrong?

HOWARD. That's not for you or me to decide, Bob. It's for her to find out. Maybe when she has her nose rubbed in the dirt a couple of afternoons, she'll emerge a normal, healthy girl.

WILSON. You realize, of course, I could stop this by expelling her.

HOWARD. Sure you could, if you'd get a kick out of demonstrating naked authority.

WILSON. Oh, I'm not going to. (*Rises. Stands by R. arm of sofa. Agnes enters down stairs, stands on them*) I don't blame Virginia. It's been my experience that in dealing with people like you, the parent is in much greater need of education than the child.

AGNES. (*Crossing down stairs to below newel post*) Well, how are we doing down here?

HOWARD. Fine, darling, just fine.

WILSON. (*Crossing L. above sofa to Agnes*) Oh, yes. The girls demand that gym be abolished. Virginia wants to play football. I have been plagued by boys who want to smoke in class. I caught two kids necking in the corridor. Because of *his* little speech my life has become a model of exquisite misery.

HOWARD. Well, Bob, the problems of modern education aren't simple, you know.

WILSON. (*In great anger, picks up his hat from table above sofa*) Agnes, it is my considered opinion that your husband is a blight on the American academic scene—(*Crosses up C. To Howard, over his shoulder*)—and a full-grown juvenile delinquent. (*Slaps hat on his head and exits to R. front door*)

HOWARD. (*Rises, laughing*) I'd better go after him. He forgot his coat.

AGNES. (*Takes coat. Crossing up to closet. Hangs coat*) Don't be silly. He won't get cold for a long time. (HOWARD *crosses L. to phone table*) I'll have one of the kids take it to school tomorrow.

HOWARD. Did you hear the way that kid talked to Bob Wilson?

AGNES. (*Crossing down to arch*) Do you think maybe Virginia really is part gazelle? (GINGER *enters down stairs, wearing football pants*)

GINGER. Mom.

AGNES. Yes, dear.

GINGER. Where's the sewing box?

AGNES. Ask Lizzie.

GINGER. (*Crossing L. to kitchen*) I've got to take a tuck in these pants. (*Exits into kitchen*)

HOWARD. (*Crosses L. to below sideboard. Calling off into kitchen*) Hold that line. (*Crosses R. a few steps*) I hope Eddie Davis tackles her so hard her teeth rattle for a week.

AGNES. (*Crossing D.L. to D.L. corner*) I hope she beats Eddie Davis out for his position, is elected Captain of the team, and makes the All American.

HOWARD. You can't make the All American till you're in college.

AGNES. Excuse me. (*Sits on D.L. corner bench*) (GINGER, *followed by Liz, enters from kitchen, glass of milk in her R. hand, holding her pants up with her L. hand, a carrot in her teeth. They walk in step,* LIZ *carrying sewing box. As* GINGER *passes Howard she makes a haughty toss of the carrot greens over her shoulder. They cross R. and up stairs. On lower landing* LIZ *makes the three ring sign to* AGNES *and exits*)

HOWARD. (*Crossing R. to foot of stairs*) Isn't that ridiculous? (AGNES *laughs*) What are you laughing at? (*Crosses down to arm-chair, sits*)

AGNES. You know perfectly well you're proud and delighted and would give your elk's tooth to see her play. (HOWARD *picks up Time magazine from drum table*)

HOWARD. You must think I'm insane.

AGNES. I do. I think you're the most wonderfully insane man I know, and I wouldn't have any one else for the father of my children.

HOWARD. I hope not. (*Laughs*) You know, this might just make the front page of the paper in the morning.

AGNES. Right next to your famous last words.

HOWARD. Oh, my gosh! (*Throws magazine in the air. As* HOWARD *rises*)

CURTAIN FALLS

ACT TWO

Scene 1
The same

At Rise: Front door slams. LIZ *enters from front door, crosses to closet, hangs up her coat.*

LIZ. Mrs. Carol.

AGNES. *(Entering from kitchen)* Liz? *(Crosses to D.R. of sideboard)*

LIZ. *(Crossing L. to Agnes)* How's the roast?

AGNES. They'll eat it. Any news?

LIZ. Not yet. They just finished their last scrimmage.

AGNES. But she must know by now whether or not she made the team?

LIZ. *(Crossing down to sofa, sits on L. arm)* No. Mr. Blake doesn't tell any one he's cut until after they hit the locker room today.

AGNES. Tell them they're what?

LIZ. Cut. When the coach walks up to you and says, "You're cut," it means you are no longer a member of the team.

AGNES. *(Taking off her apron)* How do you know all these things?

47

LIZ. I'm an authority. (AGNES *laughs, crosses up to sideboard, puts her apron down*) I've been to all the practice sessions and know every play by heart.

AGNES. So does Howard. (LIZ *rises, crosses L. to ottoman*)

LIZ. Pretty good coach, that Blake. (*Puts L. foot up on ottoman*) Fast running game from the "T" but not much razzle-dazzle.

AGNES. That's a shame.

LIZ. Good ground game. No air arm. (*Front door slams.* LIZ *steps down from ottoman*) Maybe this is her. (LIZ *and* AGNES *cross up C.* JOAN *from front door, carrying petition*)

JOAN. Hello.

LIZ. Have you heard any news?

JOAN. (*Crossing L., stops at kitchen door*) How could I? This was gym day. (*Exits into kitchen*)

LIZ. (*Looks at Agnes. Crossing L., shouting off to kitchen*) Don't you take gym during school?

AGNES. No, dear, she upholds her father's ideals by cutting gym in protest, and spends two afternoons a week in detention. She fixes them.

LIZ. (*Shouting off to kitchen*) Didn't you go over to the football field to cheer Ginger on?

JOAN. (*Off*) I most certainly did not.

LIZ. Why not?

JOAN. (*Entering from front door with coke, her coat over her arm*) The girls in the senior class have declared the football field "off limits." (*Crosses R., puts coke and petition on table behind sofa. Then crosses up to closet, hangs up coat*)

AGNES. Sounds like the senior class of 1890.

JOAN. You can laugh if you like, but if Daddy lets Ginger get on the squad we'll boycott the games. (AGNES *crosses R. to window, looks out*)

LIZ. (*Crosses down to behind drum table*) You ought to be ashamed of yourself, acting like a twelve-year old child.

JOAN. (*Crossing down to sofa*) Well, I'm not. (*Sits on C. of sofa*)

LIZ. I go down and watch every day, and let me tell you, Ginger can kick and she can run.

JOAN. We'll see how much good she does the team in the face of an economic embargo.

AGNES. Does this mean war?

LIZ. (*Starts L. toward kitchen*) Call me as soon as she comes in, Mrs. Carol. (*Front door slams*)

AGNES. All right, Liz.

LIZ. (*Turns R., crossing U. to R. of sideboard*) Maybe this is her. (JEANNIE *enters from front door, crosses L. to kitchen*)

AGNES. Hello, Jeannie.

JEANNIE. Hello.

AGNES. What's the matter?

JEANNIE. (*Off*) Nothing.

JOAN. How's the play coming?

JEANNIE. (*Entering from kitchen door with a coke in her hand, coat over her arm. She slaps kitchen door*) I hate that guy Thompson. He's nothing but an unmitigated bore. (*Crossing R., sets coke on table behind sofa and crosses up to closet, hangs coat in it*)

AGNES. (*Crossing L. to sideboard*) Jeannie.

JEANNIE. Well, he is. He says cruel, vicious, insulting things to me. Everybody laughs. (*Slams closet door*) And it's all Dad's fault. (*Crosses D.L. to Agnes*)

AGNES. How do you arrive at that, dear?

JEANNIE. (*Crossing down to L. of sofa*) If he hadn't let Ginger go out for the team, I wouldn't have had all this humiliation.

AGNES. Like what?

JEANNIE. Today Guy said, "Miss Carol, this is a love scene, not an off-tackle smash." (LIZ *crosses up to sideboard, picks up apron*)

AGNES. Oh. (JOAN *laughs*)

JEANNIE. (*Crossing R. to sofa*) It's not funny, Joan.

JOAN. I'm sorry.

JEANNIE. (*Sits on L. of sofa*) I could die. (*Front door slams*)

LIZ. (*Crossing R. to R. of sideboard;* AGNES *crosses up to R. of foot of stairs*) This must be her. (HOWARD *enters from front door with brief-case*)

AGNES. (*Standing ready for a kiss*) Hello, darling. (HOWARD *crosses D.L. slowly to behind drum table*)

JEANNIE *and* JOAN. Hello, Daddy!

LIZ. (*Crossing down to U.R. of ottoman*) Hello, Mr. Carol. Would you like some coffee?

HOWARD. (*Puts brief-case on drum table*) No, thank you. Save it for Virginia Carol, girl athlete. (JOAN *and* JEANNIE *exchange looks, then look at Howard*)

LIZ. She's not allowed to have coffee.

HOWARD. Then throw it out.

LIZ. Okay, I will. (LIZ *exits into kitchen.* HOWARD *takes bag of jelly beans from brief-case and drops it on drum table. Then takes copy of Life magazine from brief-case, hiding its cover from audience*)

AGNES. (*Crossing down to U.R. of ottoman*) How come so late, darling? (JEANNIE *and* JOAN *set down their cokes on coffee table*)

HOWARD. I was detained at the bank. Has anyone seen this? (*Holds Life magazine up, revealing its cover of Virginia in a football helmet, to the audience and to his family*)

AGNES. Oh, no! (AGNES *crosses L. to Howard, takes magazine from him. She then crosses back to C.* JEANNIE *rises, crosses L., stands L. of Agnes.* JOAN *rises, crosses L., stands R. of Agnes*)

JOAN. It's Ginger.

HOWARD. It says, "The New Look in Football." Pictures start on Page 103. (JEANNIE *and* JOAN *open magazine*) There's a whole lay-out.

JEANNIE. Isn't this exciting?

HOWARD. It's hysterical.

JOAN. Here's the page.

AGNES. That's a wonderful picture of Virginia.

HOWARD. Read what it says.

JEANNIE. (*Takes magazine. Reads*) "Virginia Carol, daughter of town banker, as she appears after a hard two-hour scrimmage."

AGNES. (*To Howard*) She could have combed her hair.

JOAN. Here's a picture of Mr. Wilson. (HOWARD *grimaces, takes off coat*)

JEANNIE. And here's a picture of the bank.

AGNES. What's this?

JOAN. Why, it's a photostatic copy of the petition against gym for girls.

JOAN *and* JEANNIE. Aw, Daddy! (*Howard takes his coat and hat, slowly crosses up to closet, hangs his coat.* JOAN *and* JEANNIE *cross R. to sofa and sit,* JOAN *in C. and* JEANNIE *on L.* AGNES *crosses R., sits on L. arm of sofa*)

JEANNIE. (*Reading*) "Petition circulated day she reported for first practice quotes banker—father who said, 'I would abolish gymnasium for girls because no one should be forced to do anything he doesn't want to do.'" (*Howard crosses down L. slowly to arm-chair, sits*) I still agree with you, Daddy.

JOAN. So do I.

JEANNIE. (*Reading*) "In a quiet, straight-laced town, a beautiful 14-year old redhead"—(*Takes*) beautiful 14-year old redhead? (AGNES *nudges Jeannie to continue reading.* JEANNIE *reads*) "—Daughter of ultra conservative banking stock—" (AGNES, JOAN *and* JEANNIE *giggle.* HOWARD *looks at them sourly*) "—kicks over the traces by reporting as a football candidate."

AGNES. Howard, have you seen this? (JOAN *takes magazine, moves R. on sofa*)

HOWARD. Yes, and so will 27 million other people this week. (JEANNIE *climbs to her knees on sofa*)

JOAN. (*Reading*) "Father, Howard G. Carol, is a victim of such remarks as, 'We'd never have to worry about depression here if he could run a bank like she can run a ball.' Rival bank has printed blotters which say . . ."

HOWARD. ". . . which say, 'if you're looking for a half-back, you've got the wrong bank.'" (AGNES, JOAN *and* JEANNIE *laugh.* HOWARD *rises, crosses up to sideboard*)

AGNES. Howard, this is fantastic.

JEANNIE. They don't even mention my playing in *Victoria*.

HOWARD. Jeannie, will you and Joan go upstairs for a few minutes? I want to talk to your mother alone.

JEANNIE. Sure. (*Rises, takes coke, crosses up to stairs, exits*)

JOAN. (*Rises*) Daddy. . . .

HOWARD. (*Crossing down to stage L. wall table*) Yes.

JOAN. (*Crossing L. to Howard*) Would you sign this petition against Ginger playing football? (AGNES *crosses down, sits on C. of sofa*)

HOWARD. Not unless you can guarantee me international notoriety.

JOAN. Very well. But it's all your fault I have to take gym twice a week. (AGNES *picks up Life from coffee table*)

HOWARD. I'm sorry. Now would you mind getting out of here for about five minutes? (*Crosses down to drum table*)

JOAN. All right. (*Crosses R. to sofa*) May I take this? (AGNES *holds magazine away from Joan*)

HOWARD. No, you may not.

JOAN. (*To Howard*) I want to read about the Movie of the Week.

HOWARD. Agnes. . . .

AGNES. Joan, will you please do as you are told.

JOAN. Very well, Mother. (*Crossing up to stairs*) But I think everybody's being very selfish.

HOWARD. About what?

JOAN. (*On lower landing*) No one's thought of what a blow these pictures will be to Eddie's morale, have they? He's only the captain of the team. (JOAN *exits up stairs.* AGNES *sets magazine down on coffee table*)

HOWARD. (*Crossing R. to L. of sofa*) Agnes, I've had a rough day.

AGNES. Down at the bank? (*Howard nods*) Because of the pictures?

HOWARD. There's one you didn't get to, on the next page. (AGNES *picks up magazine, but hesitates to turn page.* HOWARD *signals her to turn it, and she does so*)

AGNES. (*Gasps*) Howard!

HOWARD. Read what that says.

AGNES. (*Reading.* HOWARD *crosses U. as she reads*) "Virginia Carol, girl football player, and father roll around in the dirt during hard scrimmage after she had knocked him down." Howard. . . .

HOWARD. (*Crossing D.R. to sofa*) I was standing around on the field during practice a couple of weeks ago. They had an end sweep toward me at one point. She threw a block, missed the end, hit me, and down we went. (*Breaks L., then turns back*) It just happened to be the day the photographers were there.

AGNES. Oh, dear!

HOWARD. It was a bad block, too high. After it was over, she picked me up, looked me straight in the eye, and said, "Spectators." (*Takes magazine from Agnes, crosses L. to behind drum table*)

AGNES. Was she hurt, dear?

HOWARD. (*Stops*) No, darling, she got right off me. (*Puts magazine on drum table, open*)

AGNES. You weren't hurt, were you?

HOWARD. (*Crossing R., slowly*) Aside from a few minor cuts and bruises, slight giddiness, a lack of focus, and their having to carry me to a bench and give some water, I was fine. (*Crosses R. above sofa to R. of it*)

AGNES. (*Laughs silently*) Well, you're too old to be playing football anyway. What did Ed Hoffman say?

HOWARD. (*Turns to Agnes*) Nothing. He just kept looking at me—(*Shakes head*)—and shaking his head.

AGNES. What does that mean?

HOWARD. Oh, he's probably disappointed because I missed the ball carrier.

AGNES. I'm serious.

HOWARD. (*Crossing L. below coffee table to above armchair*) I don't know. He said he'd be over later to talk to me.

AGNES. Well, Ed may be president of the bank but he's got a sense of humor.

HOWARD. (*Stops*) He certainly has. (*Crossing L.*) Oh, Lord, it was just a simple little speech on manners.

AGNES. (*Rises. Crossing L. to Howard*) Well, darling, don't feel badly about it. When Virginia gets home, we'll simply explain the situation to her and that will be . . .

HOWARD. Oh, no, we won't. (*Turns to Agnes*)

AGNES. What?

HOWARD. I absolutely forbid you to tell your daughter the possible consequences of her madness.

AGNES. Now darling, that's silly.

HOWARD. I mean it. I wouldn't dream of suppressing this child.

AGNES. Howard, you're being stubborn and ridiculous.

HOWARD. That's the last word. If we lose the house we can all go down and live under the bleachers, right next to her beloved football field.

AGNES. *(Looking around R.)* And on Saturday I can sell peanuts.

HOWARD. Anyway, if I did ask her to quit, she'd probably claim I'm putting selfish interests like home, family, and security above her individual rights. *(Sits on edge of drum table)*

AGNES. *(Crossing L. to L. of Howard. Puts arms around him)* Howard, I love you.

HOWARD. Where *is* she?

AGNES. Now, darling, don't get nervous.

HOWARD. She's taking the longest way home just to keep me in suspense. *(Front door bell)* That's probably Ed Hoffman now. I was hoping she'd get here before he did, but no, she'd rather sit in some dirty old locker room. (LIZ *enters from kitchen, laughing, carrying a copy of Life, which she is reading*)

LIZ. *(Crossing R. to R. of Howard)* Oh, Mr. Carol, you're famous. (AGNES *signals Liz to "Sh"*)

HOWARD. Would you mind answering the door, Liz?

LIZ. Not at all. (LIZ *exits to front door*)

HOWARD. *(In Agnes' arms)* Oh, Agnes, why couldn't she have been a boy?

AGNES. Ohhhh . . . darling. (LIZ *enters from front door*)

LIZ. It's Mr. Hoffman. *(Crosses L. to below sideboard)* (ED HOFFMAN *enters from front door*)

ED. Hya, Howie . . . Agnes.

HOWARD. (*Rises, crossing U.R. to Ed*) Hya, Ed. Come in.

AGNES. Can I take your coat?

ED. (*Takes off coat*) No, thanks, I'll just throw it across a chair. (*Crosses D.L. to armchair, starts to drop coat over back*)

HOWARD. (*Crosses R. to Ed, takes coat from him*) I'll get it, Liz. Sit down, Ed. (*Crosses U. to hallway chair, puts coat and hat on it*)

ED. Thank you. I'm sorry, Liz.

LIZ. It's all right, Mr. Hoffman. (LIZ *exits into kitchen*)

ED. Well, Ag, how does it feel to be the wife of a national figure?

AGNES. Pretty awesome. (*Crosses R. to sofa, sits*)

ED. I'm sure. You must be very proud of him.

AGNES. I am. (HOWARD *re-enters, crosses down to behind sofa*)

ED. You certainly put this town on the map.

HOWARD. Yeah, and myself, too.

ED. Yes. (*Crossing slowly down around ottoman to armchair*) Did he tell you, since Life magazine came out people have been streaming into the bank?

AGNES. No.

ED. Not to do business, you understand, just to make jokes. (*Sits in arm chair*)

AGNES. Well, that will pass.

ED. At one point I was closing a deal with old man Bryant, and I heard what sounded like an uprising of savages in a Hollywood movie. Into the bank burst a group of our most respected merchants doing a snake dance and shouting, "Booma lacka, booma lacka, sis boom bah. Howard Carol, rah rah rah!"

AGNES. What did you do?

ED. I'm president of the bank. What could I do? (*Rises*) I rushed out of my office and got on the end of the line. (*Snake-dancing R. above table to C.*) "Booma lacka, booma lacka, sis boom bah. Howard Carol, rah, rah, rah." (*Howard sits on L. back of sofa*)

ED. I wonder what ever happened to old man Bryant? I lost him in the snake dance.

AGNES. Sounds like a Legion convention.

ED. Practically. By the way, I met Mrs. Claude Brackett on the street. She said, "Young man." You know how old she is. I said, "Yes, Mrs. Claude Brackett." She said, "What is an anarchist?" I said, "Why?" She said, "I want to know if it's dangerous."

AGNES. What does she mean by anarchist, Ed?

ED. (*Crossing L. to behind drum table*) Didn't you read Bob Wilson's statement in *Life*?

AGNES. Statement?

HOWARD. Well, he's a stuffed shirt, anyway.

ED. (*Picks up magazine*) Let me read it to you. Right under his picture they have a caption that reads, "Irate principal Robert Wilson," and then a quote which says, "I do not blame the poor child. I blame her father, who told me he would let her burn down the house." (AGNES *leans forward on sofa, stares at Howard.* HOWARD *catches her glance*)

HOWARD. No, no, he misquoted me. I said if she felt she had to do it, I might let her burn out one room in the house.

ED. Well, that's different. I knew you'd never let her burn down the whole house. (AGNES *leans back*)

AGNES. Which room?

HOWARD. Her own room.

AGNES. That's right next to ours.

HOWARD. I can't help that. Change her room.

ED. Well, that's settled. Anyway, Bob goes on to say, "Any parent who preaches anarchy to his children is either a complete idiot or has no regard for law and order. (*Crossing R. to Howard*) "In any case he hardly seems qualified to hold an advisory position at a bank."

AGNES. He has some nerve.

ED. (*Crossing R. below coffee table*) He certainly has. Every bank has to have at least one lunatic to deal with the depositors. (*Drops magazine on coffee table, crosses R. to R. of sofa*)

AGNES. Howard, I don't suppose anybody will take him seriously.

HOWARD. And if they do, they can just go jump in the river so far as I'm concerned.

ED. What are you getting so upset about?

HOWARD. I'm getting a little tired of all these jokes.

ED. It's just fun, Howie.

HOWARD. I know, but a lot of people were kidding on the level today. (TOMMY GREEN *bursts into the room from kitchen, looking back at* LIZ, *who follows him from kitchen*)

TOMMY. (*Rushing by Howard*) Hello. . . . (*Crosses R. to below foot of stairs*)

AGNES. Hello Tommy.

LIZ. (*In kitchen doorway*) He sneaked past me. (LIZ *exits into kitchen*)

TOMMY. Is Ginger home yet?

AGNES. No, she is not.

TOMMY. Do you mind if I sit and wait? (*Crosses U., sits in chair R. of phone table*)

AGNES. (*Crossing up to Tommy*) I'm sorry, Tommy, but we're having a very important discussion.

TOMMY. I'll be completely unobtrusive.

HOWARD. (*Crosses R. to Tommy*) I'm terribly sorry, but you can't stay.

TOMMY. (*Rises. To Howard*) Maybe this doesn't mean anything to you, but if Ginger makes the football team, she and I are through.

ED. (*Steps down to R. of coffee table, turns U.L. to Tommy*) Young man, do you know who I am?

TOMMY. Of course, Mr. Hoffman.

ED. If you don't go, right now, the first thing I'll do when I leave here is—(*Turning slowly front*) foreclose the mortgage on your father's house. (*Leers.* TOMMY *crosses L. fast, exits into kitchen.* ED, HOWARD *and* AGNES *laugh*)

ED. (*Crossing L. to arm chair*) Ah, kids. I've got two of my own and every day I grow to hate them more. (*Looks at Howard. Sits in armchair*) Shall we get back to our scrimmage?

HOWARD. (*Crosses down to C.*) You heard what Tommy just said. He doesn't want to have anything to do with my daughter because I let her play football.

ED. Howie, he's just a kid.

HOWARD. (*Crossing L. to ottoman*) He's probably heard a lot of other people talking like that.

ED. Don't be silly. (AGNES *crosses down to L. of sofa*)

HOWARD. That's just the beginning. (*Crossing L. to above drum table*) Now I suppose because of that idiotic statement Bob Wilson gave out, I'll be subject to all kinds of pressure.

ED. Nobody is putting any pressure on you.

HOWARD. No, not yet. But I know how these things work. One simple remark starts a whole chain reaction.

ED. You're making yourself angry.

HOWARD. (*Crossing R.*) I *am* angry.

ED. There's no reason to be.

HOWARD. (*Crossing R. to Agnes*) Maybe you don't think so, but I can see where this is leading.

ED. Where?

HOWARD. It starts with jokes. Then it develops into serious discussions. The first thing you know there is criticism, (*Crossing L. to above ottoman*) and I suppose the next thing, the board of directors will be telling me if I don't behave in a certain way, they won't renew my contract.

ED. Howie. . . .

HOWARD. Well, let me tell you that I will not change my behavior pattern to satisfy the whim of some guy like Bob Wilson.

ED. What's the matter with you?

HOWARD. And what's more, if the Board thinks I'm too irresponsible to hold an advisory position, I'll resign right now.

AGNES. (*Crossing L. to Howard*) Howard. . . .

HOWARD. (*Crossing R. above sofa to window*) I don't have to live in this town. I can go some place where people aren't so smug and provincial.

ED. Now look, Howie. I came over here to talk this over as a friend, but you're blowing it up all out of proportion.

HOWARD. I don't think so. (*Turns L.*) And what's more I don't think this is just a friendly visit.

AGNES. Now, Howard. (*Crosses R. above sofa to above Howard*)

ED. Hey, now wait a minute. (*Rises. Crossing R. to L. end of sofa*) If this is the way you're going to behave maybe we ought to examine this a little bit further.

HOWARD. I don't know what's so friendly about. . . .

ED. Just a minute. I'm not talking to you now as a friend. I'm talking to you as the president of the bank.

HOWARD. Okay, Mr. President. Let's have it. (*Sits on R. end of sofa.* AGNES *sits on R. arm*)

ED. Maybe you're right. When it was only a question of Virginia playing football, we all laughed. But if these jokes are going to make you so hot under the collar that you start to behave publicly the way you've been behaving in this room, Bob Wilson's statement is apt to seem more logical every day.

HOWARD. (*To Agnes*) Aha. What did I tell you? (*To Ed*) What do you suggest I do?

ED. All I had in mind when I came here was to suggest that you stop making any more speeches for a while. But now I suggest, first, that you stay away from the football field. Ask Barney White to print a retraction of your stand on gym for girls. And tell Virginia she can't play football. (*Crosses L. to C.*)

HOWARD. And if I won't?

ED. (*Turns R.*) Is there some great big moral issue involved here?

HOWARD. Yes, I think there is.

ED. Well, I don't. And for your own good I suggest you take my advice.

AGNES. (*Rises*) Ed, you make this sound sort of serious.

ED. I think that's entirely up to Howie. In six weeks we both have contract renewals. If Virginia's still playing football and Howie is still the clown of the town, then our bank becomes a First National Laughing place, and I don't think we can afford that.

AGNES. (*Crossing L. to Ed, above table*) Ed, if what you just described were actually to happen, where would you stand— I mean as far as Howard's concerned?

ED. Agnes, I love you both, but I'm a banker. The only thing I stand behind is money.

AGNES. Well, I certainly don't have to tell you what I think of that statement.

ED. (*Turns front*) No, and I hope you won't. (*Turns back to Agnes*) But I'm not going to tie up my security with yours over the right of Howie to pretend he's back in school, or the right of Virginia to play football.

AGNES. Now let me tell you. . . .

HOWARD. (*Rises*) Darling, would you leave Ed and me alone for a minute? (*Crosses U. and L. above sofa L. of it*)

AGNES. Sure. (*To Ed*) Excuse me. (*Crosses L., exits into kitchen*)

HOWARD. (*Crossing L. to Ed*) Ed, the reason I asked Agnes to leave us alone was so I could thank you privately for your charity and understanding in this instance.

ED. You're very welcome.

HOWARD. I don't know what kind of an old bone you or the board of directors might throw at me where you feel I can't get into any trouble. (*Crossing L. above Ed*) Why don't you lock me up in the vault in the morning and let me out at night? That way I won't have a chance to talk to anyone. (*To Ed's back*)—A sort of golden solitary confinement. (*Crosses D.L. to D.L. of drum table*)

ED. Look, Howie, this problem has a very simple solution. You're being totally unreasonable.

HOWARD. I don't think so. (*Crossing U.R. to L. of sofa*) And let me tell you I will not retract any statement I ever made. I'll say whatever I like, whenever I like. (*Crossing R. below sofa*) And what's more, under no circumstances will I ask Virginia to stop playing football.

ED. Why not?

HOWARD. (*Crossing R. below sofa to R. of it*) Because I believe everyone should be allowed to do what they want to do.

ED. Howie, she's a girl, not a boy!

HOWARD. I'm quite well aware of that fact.

ED. Sometimes I don't think you are, anymore. (*Front door slams.* GINGER *enters from it*)

HOWARD. Hello, Virginia.

GINGER. Hello, Pop. Hello, Mr. Hoffman. (*Crosses L. to stairs, starts to go up*)

ED. Hello, Virginia. (*Crosses L. to arm chair, sits*)

GINGER. (*Starting up stairs*) Excuse me.

HOWARD. (*Crossing to foot of stairs*) Virginia, did you make the team?

GINGER. I'd rather not talk about it now.

HOWARD. I'm sorry but I've got to know.

GINGER. Oh, Pop! (*She cries, turns L., away from Howard, holding on to banister.* ED *hears her cry, looks at Howard, who glares at him*)

HOWARD. Don't cry, darling.

GINGER. I can't help it. I wasn't given a fair chance. (GINGER *runs up stairs.* ED *rises, crosses R. to R. end of sofa*)

HOWARD. (*Crossing L. to kitchen door. Calling off*) AGNES. (*Crosses R. to above armchair. To Ed*) Well, there's your answer. (LIZ *enters from kitchen, followed by Agnes.* LIZ *stands above drum table,* AGNES *stands down stage of sideboard*)

AGNES. What is it?

HOWARD. Virginia's upstairs.

AGNES. Did she make the team?

HOWARD. No.

LIZ. (*Crossing R. to stairs, going up*) That's an outrage. She was the best thing on the field yesterday.

HOWARD. Just not good enough.

LIZ. She's a better half-back than most full-backs. (*Exits up stairs*)

ED. (*Crossing L. to Howard above sofa*) Well, I guess I'll be running along. So long, Howie. (*Extends R. hand to Howard*)

HOWARD. So long, Ed. (*Shakes hands with Ed, looking away from him.* AGNES *crosses R., glaring at Ed, to hall chair. She gets Ed's coat and hat, crosses down to him, hands him coat and hat. Then moves R. and stands, arms folded.* HOWARD *crosses L.*)

ED. I'm glad my little visit here didn't create any hard feelings. (ED *exits to front door*)

AGNES. (*Crossing L. to L. of Howard*) I'm so mad at Ed Hoffman, I'd like to open a bank across the street and give away money.

HOWARD. (*Crossing R. to foot of stairs*) If there is one thing I can't stand, it's unfairness. Why, she could run better than half the other kids on the field.

AGNES. You were hoping she'd get on the team, weren't you?

HOWARD. (*Crossing L. to Agnes*) You darn right, I was.

AGNES. So was I. Liz and I knelt in front of the lighted oven and prayed she'd make it. (HOWARD *pats Agnes' hand.* GINGER *enters down stairs*)

GINGER. (*Crossing down stairs to U.C.*) Pop, I want to ask you something.

HOWARD. What, darling?

GINGER. Is there a difference between boys and girls?

HOWARD. Well, in what way? (*Crosses R. to Ginger.* AGNES *follows*)

GINGER. One day I heard you say nobody takes the ball down the field as fast as me. And then the coach said I play smarter heads-up football than Eddie Davis.

HOWARD. He did, huh?

GINGER. So what I'd like to know, is it because he's a boy and I'm a girl that he made the first team, and I only made the scrub team?

HOWARD. No, no. . . . What did you say?

AGNES. You made the scrub team?

GINGER. Yes, and he made Varsity.

HOWARD. Is that what you were crying about a little while ago?

GINGER. Sure.

HOWARD. (*Arms round Ginger*) Oh, Baby, you're wonderful! Did you hear that, Ag? She made the team.

AGNES. (*Holding out R. hand as though offering peanuts. Crossing L.*) Peanuts. . . . Get your hot roasted peanuts!

CURTAIN

ACT TWO

Scene 2

At Rise: The same. A shopping bag stands against L. side of coffee table, and its contents, tied bundles of mail, are scattered on coffee table. A framed copy of Life magazine cover hangs over sideboard on wall. More bundles of mail are scattered on drum table, bench in corner D.L., and floor nearby.

Curtain rises on an empty stage. JOAN *comes down stairs carrying a big bundle of laundry. Starts toward kitchen.—Front door bell.*

JOAN *crosses back up-stage, drops laundry bundle at foot of stairs, and goes to answer bell. When she is out of sight—*

JOAN. (*Off*) Oh, thank you. (*Front door slams*)

AGNES. (*In kitchen*) Who was it, Joan?

JOAN. (*Off*) More mail. (*Enters, dragging two mail sacks*)

AGNES. (*Off*) How many sacks?

JOAN. Two.

AGNES. (*Off*) Well, you can handle that.

JOAN. (*D.R. of phone table*) Where shall I put them?

AGNES. (*Off*) Where do they look best, dear? (JOAN *stacks mail sacks one on top of the other sack in front of phone table*)

70

JOAN. (*Crossing U. to get bundle of laundry*) House work. (*Crosses L. to kitchen*) You'd think Lizzie would clean on Friday, being she insists on going to the football game every Saturday. (*Exits into kitchen*)

AGNES. (*Enters from kitchen*) Sure. (*Crosses to drum table*)

JOAN. (*Enters from kitchen. Crossing R. to foot of stairs*) Why isn't Jeannie helping today?

AGNES. (*Crossing R. to sofa*) She is an actress. Her play opens tonight and she's resting. Shall we try to do something about this fan mail?

JOAN. I don't understand why everybody in America sends Ginger letters.

AGNES. Maybe because Yale named her First Lady of the Gridiron.

JOAN. (*Crossing L. to drum table, picks up mail. Crossing L. to D.L. corner*) You'd think Daddy would stay home on Saturday to help us. (*Starts putting mail on bench in D.L. corner*)

AGNES. (*Putting mail into shopping bag. Leaves two packets on table*) How do you figure that, dear?

JOAN. If he'd kept Ginger off the squad, he and Lizzie wouldn't be at the football game today, and I would.

AGNES. I see.

JOAN. And I think he might at least assume some responsibility for changing my whole life.

AGNES. I'll tell him when he comes in.

JOAN. (*Crossing R. below armchair to C.*) Another thing I don't understand about Daddy . . .

AGNES. Joan, please relax. It's four o'clock in the afternoon. (*Crosses up behind sofa, sets shopping bag down*) What's the matter with you, anyway? (JOAN *sits C. of sofa*)

JOAN. I've got a big problem.

AGNES. (*Crossing down to sofa*) What is it?

JOAN. Well, ever since Ginger got on the football team, I've been having a lot of trouble with Eddie, every Saturday night.

AGNES. What sort of trouble? (*Sits on L. of sofa. Picks up two packets of mail from coffee table*)

JOAN. Well, it used to be we'd have a date, go to a movie or a dance, have a soda, talk awhile, and then he'd kiss me goodnight.

AGNES. And now?

JOAN. Now he wants to start kissing me goodnight as soon as we get out.

AGNES. Well, believe me when I tell you that has nothing to do with Ginger playing football. (AGNES *and* JOAN *laugh*)

JOAN. What am I going to do?

AGNES. Well, there are several things you can do. First, I'd suggest you develop a kind of attitude and not allow yourself to get into compromising situations.

JOAN. Have you ever been in the front seat of a car with a man?

AGNES. Yes, with your father.

JOAN. What did you do?

AGNES. I managed to fend him off with dignity and the illusion of superiority.

JOAN. It's kind of hard to be more superior than Eddie.

AGNES. I'm sure.—I'll tell you a little secret. I think you're going to have to bend his ego a little. Once you get the upper hand with a kid like Eddie, it's down-hill all the way.

JOAN. Suppose Eddie gets the upper hand with me?

AGNES. Oh. That's what you're really worried about, isn't it? (JOAN *nods*) Well, I know that you're intelligent enough to realize the difference between what's good and real for you, and what isn't, because if you didn't, you wouldn't be sitting here telling me your troubles.

JOAN. I guess that's right.

AGNES. There are times when that choice may be rather difficult, Joan, but speaking as a woman who knows you very well, I have absolute confidence in your judgment.

JOAN. (*Embracing Agnes*) Thanks, Mom.

AGNES. Don't worry, Joanie, everything will work out fine. (*Laughs*) And it better.

JOAN. I hope it works out like you and Daddy.

AGNES. So do I. (*Looks at bundles of mail in her hand*)

JOAN. Mom, how did you meet Daddy?

AGNES. Oh, he picked me up on the street one day.

JOAN. Mom!

AGNES. Yeah. I heard a whistle, and I turned and there was this guy. I said, "Did you whistle at me?" He nodded, and I said, "What for?"

JOAN. What did he say?

AGNES. He didn't say anything. He just put out his hand. He was holding two black jellybeans. That's how it started. He was seven and I was five.

JOAN. And you've loved him ever since?

AGNES. (*Rises. Crossing up to sideboard*) Ever since and always will. (*Puts bundles of mail into sideboard drawer.* JEANNIE *enters down stairs, to lower landing*)

JEANNIE. (*To Joan, not seeing Agnes*) Where's my mother?

AGNES. (*Crosses down three steps. Looking at Jeannie*) What? I must be tired. (JOAN *and* AGNES *laugh*)

JEANNIE. (*To Agnes*) Hello, darling.

AGNES. (*The actress*) Hello.

JOAN. (*Rises. Crossing L. to kitchen*) How's the play going to be tonight—(*Strikes pose*)—Miss Bernhardt?

JEANNIE. Guy says I look better than Helen did dress rehearsal night. (JOAN *exits into kitchen*)

AGNES. (*Crosses down to drum table*) Helen who?

JEANNIE. (*Crossing downstairs and down to U.C.*) Helen Hayes, Mother.

AGNES. Excuse me.

JEANNIE. (*Crossing L. to U.R. of armchair*) He's the most fascinating man.

AGNES. He is? Just a week ago you hated him. (*Sits in armchair*)

JEANNIE. That's before I understood the theater. He wasn't being mean, he was simply being caustic.

AGNES. Oh, I see.

JEANNIE. (*Crossing D.R., sits R. of ottoman*) He says I have all the makings of a great actress.

AGNES. He does!

JEANNIE. He says I should come to New York.

AGNES. Don't lie down on that pink cloud with those dirty shoes on.

JEANNIE. (*Sits on ottoman*) Don't you think I'll be a great actress, Mother?

AGNES. I'll come backstage tonight and tell you, Jeannie. (JOAN *enters from kitchen, carrying a coke*) One thing I do think, is you and your sister show very poor taste in not being at the football game today. (JEANNIE *rises, crosses R. to sofa*)

JEANNIE. Oh, no!

JOAN. (*Crossing down to above drum table, gives Agnes coke*) Nobody goes to the games this year.

AGNES. Thank you, Joan. You're wrong. Your father tells me the stands are packed every week, and most people come just to see your sister kick a ball around before the game begins.

JEANNIE. (*Turns L.*) They'll get tired of that when she doesn't play.

AGNES. Are those grapes terribly sour, girls?

JEANNIE. (*Crossing L. to ottoman*) Anyway, it's all Daddy's fault we can't see the games.

AGNES. What? (*Puts coke down on table*)

JEANNIE. If he hadn't let Ginger play, we juniors would be allowed to go.

JOAN. That's right.

AGNES. Now listen just a minute, girls. Joan, when you thought that gymnasium for girls was being abolished your father allowed you to give up the part in the play, didn't he?

JOAN. Yes.

AGNES. Jeannie, he allowed you to play in *Victoria*, didn't he?

JEANNIE. Yes, Mother.

AGNES. So, basically you were both permitted your free pursuits. Is that right? (JEANNIE *and* JOAN *nod Yes.* AGNES *rises, crosses up R. of Jeannie*) Then why do you feel that your father is wrong in not denying Virginia the same right you had? (*Picks up shopping bag behind sofa.* JEANNIE *crosses R. to L. of Agnes*)

JOAN. (*Crossing R. to C.*) We don't believe a girl should be allowed to play football.

JEANNIE. It's just not right, Mother.

AGNES. In other words, anything you disagree with is wrong **and** should be stopped. Is that it?

JOAN. Well, not exactly that.

AGNES. Exactly what?

JEANNIE. Well, we feel Ginger should be allowed to do whatever she wants to do, as long as it's not playing football. (AGNES *crosses L. above armchair to D.L. corner, carrying shopping bag*)

JOAN. (*Looks at Jeannie. Crossing L. to behind armchair*) That's the resolution passed by the girls of the senior and junior classes.

AGNES. By majority vote?

JEANNIE. Of course, Mother.

AGNES. I see. By democratic procedure, you have both decided to tear up the Bill of Rights. That's very interesting. (*Puts shopping bag on bench D.L. corner*)

JOAN. (*Crosses L. two steps*) Mother, we haven't.

AGNES. If you hadn't, you'd defend Virginia's right to play whether you disagreed with it or not. (JOAN *crosses R. to behind armchair*) Any questions? (*Crosses R., picks up coke bottle from drum table. Crosses R. to between* JEANNIE *and* JOAN) You know you could both take a very good lesson from your father. He stands to lose his job, but he'd rather take that chance than deprive your sister of her freedom of choice.

JEANNIE. Gee! Daddy is a kind of Joan of Arc character. Isn't he?

AGNES. (*Crossing down to armchair. Sits*) Yeah. Voices and all.

JEANNIE. (*Crossing D.R. to L. arm of sofa*) Well, from now on, I'm going to the games.

JOAN. Jeannie!

JEANNIE. I'm going over to Ginger's side, and if Eddie Davis makes one more remark about her or Dad, I'll kick him all over the school. (AGNES *takes shoes off*)

JOAN. What?

JEANNIE. He started this whole thing about the boycott because he was mad at Ginger.

JOAN. (*Crossing R. to Jeannie*) Well, why shouldn't he be?

JEANNIE. Why should he be?

JOAN. She ruined his prestige as captain of the track team.

JEANNIE. Well, from now on, I go along with Ginger.

JOAN. How dare you?

AGNES. All right, girls, that's enough. Go to a neutral corner. (JOAN *crosses L. to behind drum table*)

JEANNIE. You're upsetting me emotionally, and I have a performance tonight. (*Sweeps around to R., exits up stairs*)

JOAN. (*Over Agnes's L. shoulder*) She's a traitor to American womanhood, per se. (JOAN *exits into kitchen*)

AGNES. (*Putting shoes on*) It was a simple little speech on manners!

HOWARD. (*Off U.R.*) Agnes.

AGNES. Yes, dear.

HOWARD. (*Off U.R.*) Agnes. (*Front door slams and* HOWARD

enters, wearing raccoon coat and felt hat pushed back on his head) Where is she? (*Crosses down to U.L. of sofa*)

AGNES. Where is who?

HOWARD. My daughter.

AGNES. (*Rises*) Which one?

HOWARD. (*Crossing up to stairs. Yells up*) Ginger! Ginger!

AGNES. (*Crossing up R. to C.*) Good Lord, what's happened to you?

HOWARD. (*Crossing down to Agnes*) I tore down the goal posts.

AGNES. Why?

HOWARD. You mean you haven't heard?

AGNES. No.

HOWARD. (*Takes Agnes in his arms*) She scored a touch-down in the last two minutes of play.

AGNES. What did they do, throw her over the goal post?

HOWARD. Sit down and let me tell you all about it.

AGNES. (*Crossing D.R. to sofa*) Try and stop you. (HOWARD *takes off coat and hat, puts them over back of armchair*) Are you going to start from the opening kick-off? (*Sits on C. of sofa*)

HOWARD. No, just the last two minutes.

AGNES. What happened before that?

HOWARD. Nothing. That's the first time she got in the game.

AGNES. Howard, either you're coloring this or it was an awfully dull afternoon.

HOWARD. Please, dear, let me talk.

AGNES. Carry the ball.

HOWARD. (*C.*) It was the last two minutes of the game. The Varsity 11 was playing its heart out down on the field. We had possession of the ball on our own thirty-yard line. It was the third down and four to go. Should they run it for the four yards, or should they—(*Gestures*)—throw a pass, with their backs to the goal?

AGNES. Run it.

HOWARD. They elected to kick.

AGNES. They're so young, didn't you know they would?

HOWARD. (*Points D.L.*) The kick went deep into coffin corner.

AGNES. Where's that?

HOWARD. The two-yard line.

AGNES. Why do they call it the coffin corner?

HOWARD. (*Crossing D.L. to below armchair*) Agnes, please!

AGNES. All right, so it's down in coffin corner. Now what?

HOWARD. The enemy takes possession. He smashes at the line. No gain. Second and ten on their own two. What should they do? (*Crossing U.L. to above drum table*) The right half drops back into the end zone, and shoots a long pass out into the flat. Three men are down there. It looks like it will be completed, but Eddie Davis smashes through and knocks it down.

AGNES. Good old Eddie!

HOWARD. Third and ten. Now what? The right half takes it on a wide end sweep. He's going wide, wide. The end is out. It looks like the ball carrier is in the clear, but no. . . .

AGNES. No?

HOWARD. No! They bring him down with a yard loss.

AGNES. I thought he was going to break through.

HOWARD. Yeah, everybody did. (*Crosses R. to L. of sofa*) Okay, it's the fourth and ten.

AGNES. Fourth and eleven! They just lost a yard.

HOWARD. Yeah. You're getting good. (*Crosses R. and pats Agnes's back. Crosses back to C.*) Okay, they're going to kick. They go into punt formation.

AGNES. Where's your daughter?

HOWARD. On the bench.

AGNES. Howard, there's not much time left.

HOWARD. (*Crossing L. to above drum table, rubbing hands*) Yeah, isn't it wonderful? (*Crossing R. to C.*) Okay, they're going to kick. Suddenly the whistle blows. Our team calls a time-out. (*Crouches down*) They go back into a huddle. The fans sense something momentous is going to happen. One man breaks away from the huddle and—(*Points L.*)—trots towards the bench. It's Eddie Davis, the Captain. The crowd cheers, he was pretty good today. (*Crossing L. to above drum table*) But who are they putting in his place?

AGNES. Whom!

HOWARD. My daughter! (*Crosses L. to U.L. of drum table. Then, trotting down stage R. and U. to C.*) She trots away from the bench, across the field. The fans go mad. They scream, they whistle, they cheer. They're yelling, (*Shaking his fists and jumping in the air*) "It's *her*. It's *her*!" (*Crosses D. to R. of ottoman*) I am completely calm and silent.

AGNES. I can just imagine!

HOWARD. (*Crossing up to C.*) Now I know we will see some football. The referee greets her . . . she greets him. . . .

AGNES. At least they're on friendly terms.

HOWARD. (*Goes into a huddle*) She joins the circle of her teammates. They're glad she is in the game.

AGNES. Howard, get to the play!

HOWARD. Don't you want the mood?

AGNES. No.

HOWARD. Okay. Fourth and eleven. They're going to kick. (*Points Upstage*) My daughter is sent back to the safety position to receive the punt. (*Crosses D. to below ottoman*) The ball is— (*Indicates*)—snapped. He gets the—(*Indicates*)—kick away. (*Crosses U. to C.*) It's a long one, down the field, past the fifty-yard line. (*Backing up to newel post of stairway*) She's going back, back! (*Indicates receiving kick*) She takes it in her own territory and starts up the field. The ends try to box her in but she slips them, and starts for the right side. The stands are on their feet. She has no interference. (*At L. end of sofa*) She's at the fifty, the forty, she shakes off a tackler at the thirty-five. She's down to the thirty, and is trapped.

AGNES. Big boys?

HOWARD. (*Through cupped hands*) Reverse your field, I scream. (*Stamping foot four times*) Reverse your field! (*Direct to Agnes*) She hears me, (*Crosses U.*) cuts back to the thirty-five, (*Crosses L.*) swings over to the left side, (*Crosses U.*) crosses back to the center, and streaks off into the clear, with only three men between her and the goal line.

AGNES. Three men?

HOWARD. (*Crossing D. three steps slowly, grimacing*) They start up after her. (AGNES *puts hands over her face*) They think they've got her in a trap—(*Stops*) But she doesn't yield. She tries to feint them out of position, but they keep coming. Suddenly she does a—(*Spins up R.*)—half spin, (*Crosses down L.*) straight-arms a man, (*Side-steps R.*) hurdles the man who tries to knock her out of bounds, and then—(*Prances down stage*)—dances down the side-line stripe and—(*Goes down on his knees*)—over the goal-line for a touch-down. (*Kisses floor*) Pay dirt!

AGNES. Well, I'm glad that's over.

HOWARD. (*Sits up*) No-o-o, then the extra point!

AGNES. (*Puts hands over her ears*) I don't want to hear about that.

HOWARD. What a game, what a game! (*Falls back on floor*) I'm exhausted. (*Sits up*) After it was over the team carried her around on their shoulders. The crowd surged out onto the field and that modest little hero kept shouting, "Put me down! Put me down!"

AGNES. Did they?

HOWARD. At last. Agnes, I don't want you to feel you've completely missed one of the great moments in the history of this town.

AGNES. Don't worry, dear, I'm certain we shall relive that moment many times. (HOWARD *laughs*) And as the years roll by, it will get even more graphic.

HOWARD. (*Rises*) Anyway, I've brought you something.

AGNES. Jellybeans!

HOWARD. A piece of that historic goal post. (*Takes small piece of wood from pocket, hands it to Agnes*)

AGNES. I shall treasure this always.

HOWARD. (*Reaches for piece of wood*) You don't have to take it if you don't want to.

AGNES. (*Holding it away from Howard*) No, no. I wouldn't be without it.

HOWARD. (*Crossing L. to drum table. Picks up coke*) He's a shrewd man, that Blake.

AGNES. He's shrewd?

HOWARD. One of the smartest coaches I've ever known.

AGNES. That's interesting.

HOWARD. (*Crosses U.R. to above armchair*) Do you realize what he's been doing these past two weeks?

AGNES. No, I'm afraid I don't.

HOWARD. He's been keeping her under wraps. (*Drinks coke*)

AGNES. Well, it's been getting awfully cold, Howard.

HOWARD. (*Crosses U. to sideboard, slams coke down on it. Cross-*

ing R. to C.) What is the use of talking to you! "Under wraps" means he's kept her on the bench because he didn't want anybody to know how good she was.

AGNES. (*Rises. Crossing L. to Howard*) Why not?

HOWARD. Because if they didn't know, she's a secret weapon.

AGNES. That's very clever.

HOWARD. Oh, golly, I wonder where that kid learned to run like that?

AGNES. (*Crossing D.L. to L. of Howard*) I used to be able to run.

HOWARD. (*Crossing down to Agne*s) Yeah, I remember. (*Embraces her*)

AGNES. Now, Howard, suppose the children come through here.

HOWARD. I think the kids know about us by now. (*Kisses Agnes. Urging Agnes R. to sofa*) I haven't been this excited since you and I were eighteen.

AGNES. (*Stops*) I was sixteen. (HOWARD *sits on C. of sofa, Agnes to his L.*)

HOWARD. I think you're more attractive now than you were then. (*Embraces Agnes*)

AGNES. You do?

HOWARD. I certainly do. (*Arm round Agnes*)

AGNES. I wish Virginia played football every day.

HOWARD. Do we have to go to that play tonight?

AGNES. We certainly do.

HOWARD. Let's come right home after it's over.

AGNES. Darling, it's a very long play.

HOWARD. Oh. Where are the kids now?

AGNES. All over. (JOAN *enters from kitchen, looks at her parents. Crosses R. to U.C. Agnes jumps up, crosses R. to mirror, fixes hair. Then crosses up to U.R. of sofa. Howard spots a piece of lint on carpet to R. of coffee table and bends over to pick it up*) Feeling better?

JOAN. Uh-huh. Hello, Daddy.

HOWARD. Hya, beautiful. Did you hear about the game today?

JOAN. No.

HOWARD. Well, it was the last two minutes of play. Your sister . . .

AGNES. (*To Howard*) Howard, you're going to get all excited again. (*Looks up, sees Joan*)

JOAN. Excuse me. (*Crosses U., goes up stairs to lower landing*) Oh, Mom.

AGNES. Yes?

JOAN. Thanks for the advice. (*Exits up stairs*)

HOWARD. (*Rises. Crosses U. to the framed Life picture hanging on wall, Agnes crosses down around coffee table and L. to D.L. corner*)
Fight 'em, Ginger,
Fight 'em, fight 'em.

Beat 'em, Ginger,
Beat 'em, beat 'em.
Rush right down that field like thunder.
(*Rushes L. toward Agnes.* AGNES *sees him coming, runs L. to D.L., protesting*)
Show them that you are a wonder!
(HOWARD *catches Agnes, embraces her.* LIZ *enters from front door, crosses down to L. of sofa*)

LIZ. Mrs. Carol. Mrs. Carol. Have you heard about the—(*Sees Agnes and Howard embracing*) Oh, excuse me. (HOWARD *breaks away from Agnes*)

AGNES. It's all right, Liz. We have no secrets.

LIZ. (*Crossing L. to C.*) Did you hear the news?

AGNES. I've been through it.

HOWARD. (*Crossing R. to Liz*) I told her, Liz, but she doesn't know anything about football.

LIZ. Isn't it wonderful, and wasn't she cute?

HOWARD. Cute? (*Picks up Liz*) She was magnificent!

LIZ. She certainly was. (*Howard puts Liz down*)

AGNES. This certainly has been an emotional experience.

HOWARD. You know what Blake will do with her now, Liz?

AGNES. Put her back under wraps, I hope.

HOWARD. Exactly, if he doesn't need her. He'll probably save her for the traditional Thanksgiving Day game. (*Running down around drum table and U.R. to foot of stairs, singing*)

Fight 'em, Ginger,
Fight 'em, fight 'em.
Beat 'em, Ginger,
Beat 'em, beat 'em. Oh, Liz.
   (*Stops at foot of stairs*)

LIZ. Yes?

HOWARD. Hang up my coat. (*Exits up stairs, running and singing*)
Run right down that field like thunder.
Show them that you are a wonder!

LIZ. (*Picks up Howard's coat from back of armchair. Crossing U.C.*) I've never seen him so happy. (*Puts coat and hat down on hallway chair*)

AGNES. I guess that counts for something.

LIZ. (*Crossing L. to above drum table*) Did he tell you everything that happened this afternoon?

AGNES. Everything.

LIZ. (*Crossing L.*) Would you like to hear my version?

AGNES. No, thank you. (*Front door slams,* GINGER *enters from front door*) Hello, baby. (*Crosses R. to below phone table*)

GINGER. (*Crossing D. to behind L. end of sofa, taking off coat*) Hello, Mom. (*Throws coat over L. back of sofa.* AGNES *and* LIZ *exchange looks*)

LIZ. Hello, Virginia.

GINGER. Hello, Liz.

AGNES. What's the matter?

GINGER. Nothing.

LIZ. (*Looks at Agnes, then at Ginger*) Ginger, you were wonderful. (*Looks at Agnes, then crosses L. below Agnes to kitchen door, where she takes one more look at Agnes, and exits to kitchen*)

AGNES. (*Crossing R. to C.*) I've just had an excited recounting of your adventure.

GINGER. Where is Pop?

AGNES. He's upstairs. (GINGER *looks upstairs, then crosses D. to sofa*) What's the matter, baby?

GINGER. Everything. (*Sits on C. of sofa*)

AGNES. But you scored a touch-down this afternoon.

GINGER. Oh, Mom, I'm miserable.

AGNES. (*Crossing R. to sofa. Sits next to Ginger*) Darling, what happened? (*Puts arm around Ginger*)

GINGER. Well, the last few seconds of the game the boys called time out. They wanted me to play, so they told Eddie to walk off quietly or they'd throw him off bodily. They knew the other team had to punt. The kicker went back to his end zone. Our line crashed through. He had to rush the kick. It was a bad punt that wobbled down to the twenty. They let me take it, then opened a hole up the center that a slow freight could have gone through. They were determined I'd score.

AGNES. Well, isn't that the purpose of the game?

GINGER. But, Mom, they all treated me like something special, not just like anybody carrying the mail.

AGNES. What about those three men who had you trapped?

GINGER. When I got to them, I slowed up. By that time I didn't want the touch-down. I wanted them to tackle me.

AGNES. And they didn't?

GINGER. They were laughing so hard, they fell flat on their faces. I had to score.

AGNES. But didn't that touch-down win the game?

GINGER. Mom . . .

AGNES. That's what I understood.

GINGER. By the time I got into the game we were leading thirty-four to nothing.

AGNES. (*Looks around upstairs, then looks front*) Well, I've been had!

GINGER. (*Rises, crosses L. to C.*) Then they picked me up on their shoulders, like a curio, and marched me around the field. Both teams. With Daddy leading them. I was furious. I kept shouting, "Put me down! Put me down!"

HOWARD. (*Off*) Do I hear the small voice of my great conquering hero?

GINGER. Yes, Pop. (*Crosses L. to behind armchair. Holds on to armchair, facing front*)

AGNES. Stand your ground, dear, or he'll run right through you.

HOWARD. (*Off*)
Fight 'em, Ginger,
Fight 'em, fight 'em.

Beat 'em, Ginger,
Beat 'em, beat 'em.

(*Enters down stairs to lower landing*) There's the little star. Five feet two-and-a-half inches of greased lightning. Welcome home, son. (GINGER *hears, runs off to kitchen*)

AGNES. (*Rises*) Son? (*Crosses L. to kitchen*) Howard!

CURTAIN

ACT THREE

The Same

At Rise: HOWARD *is seated in armchair, writing on pad of* paper.

HOWARD. (*Reading*) "Mayor Green, Commissioners, Ladies and Gentlemen. No, no. Mayor Green, Principal Wilson, Commissioners, Ladies and Gentlemen."

AGNES. (*Off*) Lizzie. . . . Lizzie. . . . Howard.

HOWARD. Yes, dear?

AGNES. (*Off*) Howard, where's Lizzie?

HOWARD. In the kitchen, I guess.

AGNES. (*Off*) Would you call her, please?

HOWARD. Lizzie.

LIZ. (*In kitchen*) What do you want, Mr. Carol?

HOWARD. What do you want, Agnes?

AGNES. (*Off*) Ask Liz if Jeannie's petticoat is pressed.

HOWARD. Liz, is Jeannie's petticoat pressed?

LIZ. (*Off*) Yes, it is.

HOWARD. Yes, it is.

AGNES. (*Off*) Oh, that's good. Would you bring it up, darling?

HOWARD. Why can't Liz bring it up?

AGNES. (*Off*) She's busy.

HOWARD. Can't you come down?

AGNES. (*Off*) I'm getting dressed.

HOWARD. (*Rises. Crossing up to foot of stairs*) Look, Agnes, I'm trying to write a speech.

AGNES. (*Off*) This is more important.

JOAN. (*Off*) Will you get my dress, too, Daddy?

HOWARD. Why can't you come down and get your own dress?

AGNES. (*Off*) Howard, you're wasting time.

JOAN. (*Off*) I'll come half way. (JOAN *and* AGNES *giggle, off.* HOWARD *crosses L. to kitchen, tossing pencil on drum table and echoing the women's laughter as he exits into kitchen. He re-enters, carrying petticoat and Joan's dress on hangers as Joan enters down stairs to lower landing, brushing her hair.* HOWARD *crosses R. to foot of lower landing and hands Joan clothes over railing*)

JOAN. Thank you, Daddy.

HOWARD. (*Crossing down to armchair*) You're welcome.

JOAN. Hey, that's a real smooth suit.

HOWARD. (*Stops*) It should be. I've been wearing it for years. (JOAN *laughs, exits up stairs.* HOWARD *sits in armchair, picks up pad, resumes writing. Door bell*)

AGNES. (*Off*) Howard, would you please answer the front door?

HOWARD. (*Puts pad and pencil down on drum table. Rises. Crossing R. to answer door*) I don't know why. I'm always the first one dressed. (HOWARD *exits to front door*)

VOICE. (*Off*) Mr. Carol's residence?

HOWARD. (*Off*) Yeah. Oh, thank you. Here you go. (*Front door slams and Howard re-enters carrying corsage box*)

AGNES. (*Off*) Who was it, dear?

HOWARD. Nobody.

AGNES. (*Off*) It must have been somebody.

HOWARD. It was the florist. (*Sets corsage box on phone table, open. Starts to cross down to armchair*)

AGNES. (*Off. Giggles*) I knew it was somebody. (HOWARD *stands C., silently counts to ten. Then crosses down to armchair, sits.* AGNES *enters down stairs, carrying small white towel in which is wrapped nail polishing equipment*)

AGNES. (*On stairs*) Howard.

HOWARD. Yes, dear. (*Turns and sees Agnes. Rises*) Hey, you look sensational.

AGNES. Thanks. (*Crosses down stairs and down to coffee table. Puts nail kit on table*) It's probably the last dress I'll be able to afford. (HOWARD *sits on R. arm of armchair*)

HOWARD. Hey, come here. (AGNES *crosses L. to Howard.* HOWARD *puts arms around Agnes*) I think you are more attractive than any of our kids.

AGNES. You do?

HOWARD. I certainly do. Say, do we have to go to that play tonight?

AGNES. (*Breaking embrace, crossing U. a few steps*) Howard. . . . (HOWARD *sits in armchair, resumes writing.* AGNES *crosses L. to over Howard's L. shoulder, looks at speech*) Darling, I don't like to invade your fantasy but how much further away from the bank is that speech going to take you?

HOWARD. Stop worrying, darling.

AGNES. (*Crossing R. to R. of ottoman*) What I don't understand is, the bank is probably furious—what makes you so happy?

HOWARD. I got a wife who loves me and the prettiest half-back ever to put on football equipment.

AGNES. (*Crossing R. two steps*) Howard, that prettiest half-back is a very unhappy little girl.

HOWARD. Oh, darling, you exaggerate things.

AGNES. (*Crosses a step R.*) *I* exaggerate things? You don't think calling her "son" this afternoon was a slight exaggeration?

HOWARD. I'm sure she understands I was excited and it just slipped out.

AGNES. (*Crossing L. to ottoman*) Don't you think it would be wise if you went upstairs and tried to explain that to her? I don't think she's even going to the play.

HOWARD. All right, darling, I will. And don't worry. Everything's going to be all right.

AGNES. My intuition tells me "No." (*Front door bell*)

HOWARD. Why does your intuition always have to be so negative?

AGNES. (*Crossing up to answer front door*) It had a very unhappy childhood. (*Off*) Hello, Ed. (HOWARD *hears, rises, quickly crosses L. to D.L. corner. Sits on bench, begins painting ceramic on potter's wheel*)

ED. (*Off*) Hello, Ag.

AGNES. (*Off*) Come in. (ED *enters from front door, followed by Agnes. Crosses L. to below phone table; she stands to his R.* ED *looks at Howard, who ignores him. Then looks back at Agnes*)

ED. Is your husband at home?

AGNES. (*Crossing down to sofa. Sits C.*) Ed's here to drop the other shoe, dear.

HOWARD. Hello, Ed.

ED. Hya, Howie.

HOWARD. Sit down. I'll be with you in a minute.

ED. (*Crossing down to L. of sofa*) You're very kind. (*Takes off his coat, drapes it over L. back of sofa*) Well, Ag, how are you?

AGNES. I don't know, but I hate being called Ag.

ED. Phyllis hates being called Phyl. Insists the children call her Phyllis. I hate being called Edward. (*Crossing L. to Howard. To Howard*) Human nature is a funny thing.

AGNES. How true. (ED *glances back at Agnes*)

ED. (*Observing Howard painting ceramic*) Occupational therapy? (HOWARD *and* AGNES *laugh*)

HOWARD. What's on your mind, Ed?

ED. All kinds of things. Tonight I was sitting around reminiscing about the scenes of my childhood. And were they harrowing! Remember them?

HOWARD. I certainly do.

ED. I said to Phyllis, "Phyl. . . . Phyl—(*Crosses down R. to drum table*)—Phyllis, I'm talking to you. Thank you. Remember the kid who failed English 2 because he turned in a paper expounding the economics of whatever it was?" (HOWARD *laughs*) She said, "Hmmmm." I said, "Whatever happened to him?" She said, "He married that handsome Hosenmacher girl." (*To Howard*) I said, "Oh, Howie Carol."

HOWARD. Yeah, Howie Carol.

ED. (*To "Phyllis" again*) I said, "Well, he made a great success today at the football game." She said, "Oh, is he back in school?" (*To Howard*) I said, "I guess so." (*Crosses L. to Howard*) Here are your contracts. (*Hands Howard contracts, which he takes from pocket*) The Board meets Tuesday. I don't think it will do much good, but sign them and turn them in. We'll see what happens.

HOWARD. Okay, thanks, Ed.

ED. Don't be so casual. I talked to some of the boys. If you are still running wild on Monday and Virginia's still on the team, you may not get approval.

HOWARD. Then there's no sense leaving the contracts, Ed, because we both will be.

ED. Howie, you made a one-man show of yourself this afternoon.

AGNES. How do you mean, Ed?

ED. (*Crossing R. to C.*) Well, first of all, he didn't sit in the stands with the people. He sat on the bench with the squad.

HOWARD. The coach invited me.

ED. When Virginia got into the game, he warmed up with her, running up and down the side-lines. He led cheers. He even tried a back flip and landed flat on his raccoon coat. When she took the ball—(*Crossing L.*)—he ran the whole thirty yards with her and was waiting for her in the end zone. (*Crossing R. to C.*) Took *her* in his arms, and kissed the left half-back.

HOWARD. What a game! What a game!

ED. I turned to say something to Barney White—he was rolling in the aisle. (*Crossing L. to Howard*) Later at the club I talked to Barney. He showed me a picture he was going to print Monday morning of Howard tearing down the goal post. Howie, you're becoming a character. More people will be coming to the games to see you than her.

HOWARD. You're just jealous, Ed.

ED. (*To Agnes*) Jealous! (*To Howard*) I'm jealous. Yes, I'm jealous. I'm jealous because little kids don't point at me on the street and go. . . . (*Points at Howard, jumps up and down, laughs*)

HOWARD. I'm sorry, Ed, but I believe everyone is entitled to the sanctity of his own privacy.

ED. Privacy? (*To Agnes*) There were twelve thousand people at that game today.

HOWARD. You know what I mean, Ed.

ED. Is that why you agreed to make a speech at the football dinner next week? What's so private about that?

HOWARD. I don't want to argue with you, Ed.

ED. You know, Ag, he's really beginning to worry me.

AGNES. Why, Ed?

ED. Any man who can construct a whole crusade on absolutely nothing is either crazy or so far ahead of his time, none of us understands him. (*To Howard*) Is everybody wrong except you?

HOWARD. Could be.

ED. (*Points to Agnes*) Talk it over with Ag. (*Crossing R. to sofa*) I'll pick you up in my car later and we'll go to the play. (*Picks up his coat, puts it on*) It may help if we're seen together. (*To Agnes*) You've been like a little mouse. See you later, Ag.

AGNES. All right, Edward.

ED. (*Hat over heart, singing*) Boola, boola. Boola, boola. (*Starting to front door*) Howie Carol, you're a foola. (*Exits front door*)

AGNES. (*Rises, crosses L. to C.*) Howard, I admire your integrity. I always like the way you feel on small important issues.

HOWARD. Thanks. What is there about me you don't admire? (*Rises, crosses R. to Agnes*)

AGNES. I hate putting maternal instincts and security above your honor, but Ed's right.

HOWARD. (*Crosses R. to armchair, puts contracts on drum table*) No, darling.

AGNES. Howard, I understand you've been hurt, but you're being proud and unwise. You heard what Ed said.

HOWARD. Ed Hoffman doesn't frighten me.

AGNES. He frightens *me*.

HOWARD. Did you see how upset he got? He doesn't want to lose me. He knows he'll be left holding the bag.

AGNES. With *us* in it.

HOWARD. No.

AGNES. Darling, would you take the advice of a life-long friend and sign those contracts?

HOWARD. (*Turns R. to Agnes*) You mean you agree with Ed?

AGNES. Yes.

HOWARD. Well, you're both wrong.

AGNES. In this discussion there are seeds that will blossom into a real quarrel.

HOWARD. Not tonight. (*Goes to grab Agnes*)

AGNES. (*Breaks R.*) You'll find out.

HOWARD. (*Crossing R. to Agnes*) Now, darling—(*Ginger appears on stairs wearing a bathrobe and slippers, carrying Jeannie's cape*)

GINGER (*Crosses down to foot of stairs*) Mom . . . look. . . . (GINGER *crosses D.R. around sofa to D.R. of Agnes. Agnes and Howard watch as* JEANNIE *enters down stairs dressed as young Queen Victoria*)

JEANNIE. Hello.

HOWARD. Well, . . . Your Highness!

AGNES. Oh, Jeannie!

JEANNIE. (*Crossing down stairs to U.C.*) You like it, Daddy?

HOWARD. It's majestic, isn't it, darling? (HOWARD *turns Jeannie around, then crosses up to phone table for corsage*)

GINGER. I helped her dress, Mom.

AGNES. You did? (*Puts arm round Ginger*)

GINGER. Uh-huh. I was her lady-in-waiting. (*Hands Agnes Jeannie's cape*)

HOWARD. (*Presenting corsage to Jeannie*) Your majesty. (HOWARD *kisses Jeannie.* GINGER *crosses L. slowly to chair in D.L. corner, and sits, observing the scene*)

JEANNIE. (*Taking flowers. Curtseys*) Thank you.

HOWARD. Kitten, you look enchanting. (*Pats Jeannie. Calling off to kitchen*) Lizzie. (*To Jeannie*) You nervous?

JEANNIE. Something's happened to my stomach. (LIZ *enters from kitchen dressed for play. Crosses R. to D.C. near sideboard*)

LIZ. Did you call me, Mr. Carol? (HOWARD, JEANNIE, *and* AGNES *ad lib admiration*)

AGNES. (*Crossing U. to D.R. of Jeannie*) Liz, we called you in to take a look at our little star, but I'm not sure you're not more attractive. (*Winks at Ginger*)

LIZ. I always dress for opening nights.

HOWARD. (*Crossing L. to Liz*) We have so many here in town. (*Hands Liz keys*) Here are the keys to the car, Liz. (*Helps Liz on with cape*) Don't worry about getting it back. We're going down with Ed Hoffman.

AGNES. I'll take the car out of the garage for you, Lizzie.

LIZ. Okay. (*Crosses R. to above ottoman. To Jeannie*) Are you ready? (JEANNIE *looks at Liz, who crosses R. to below R. corner of arch*)

JEANNIE. Uh-huh.

AGNES. Good luck, now. (*Kisses Jeannie*)

JEANNIE. Thank you. (AGNES *begins hooking Jeannie's cape*) Mom, just a couple of very important things. Don't forget to applaud the scenery when the curtain goes up. Guy says that's important. Only don't applaud me when I first come on the stage, just because I'm the star of the play. He says that's amateurish. Even Helen Hayes insists they don't applaud her.

LIZ. What does she do, hold up her hands? (GINGER's *head drops down*)

JEANNIE. (*To Liz*) If they applaud, she kills it.

AGNES. Kills what?

JEANNIE. (*Turns L. to Agnes*) Don't you know what that means?

AGNES. No, dear, I don't.

JEANNIE. Neither do I, but Guy does.

LIZ. Anything else?

JEANNIE. (*To Liz*) Yes. There are some places where you're not supposed to laugh, but I don't have time to tell you about them now.

AGNES. We'll sit very quietly.

JEANNIE. But there are other places where you are supposed to laugh.

HOWARD. We'll watch the other people.

AGNES. Be awfully regal, Jeannie. (*Embraces Jeannie*)

JEANNIE. I will. (*Crossing L. to Howard*) Bye, Daddy.

HOWARD. Bye, kitten. And remember what I told you—don't lope. (*Kisses Jeannie.* AGNES *crosses U.C.*)

JEANNIE. I won't. (JEANNIE *exits through front door, head high.* AGNES *looks at Howard, follows Jeannie off*)

LIZ. (*Crosses up to C.*) Makes me feel like the Dowager Queen. (*Exits.* HOWARD *turns L., sees Ginger sitting in small chair D.L., stops a moment. Crosses down to armchair.* GINGER *rises, crosses U.R. as though to exit up stairs*)

HOWARD. Virginia. . . . (*Sits in armchair*)

GINGER. (*Stops below phone table*) Yes, Pop?

HOWARD. (*Holding R., hand out*) Come here. (GINGER *croses down to Howard, hands behind back*) You mad at me?

GINGER. No.

HOWARD. I'm sorry I called you "son" this afternoon.

GINGER. That's all right, Pop.

HOWARD. What's the matter?

GINGER. Nothing, Pop.

HOWARD. Oh, sure there is. Come on, tell me. (GINGER *sits on ottoman next to armchair*)

GINGER. I don't know, Pop. I feel kind of funny and unhappy.

HOWARD. I think maybe I know what that is.

GINGER. You do? What?

HOWARD. Growing pains. Every kid goes through that.

GINGER. Did you go through it?

HOWARD. Sure. When I was your age I felt funny all the time. (GINGER *smiles*)

GINGER. Pop, when you were my age didn't you ever have dates?

HOWARD. Only with your mother.

GINGER. Did you take long walks together and just talk?

HOWARD. No. I wasn't much of a talker then.

GINGER. What did you do?

HOWARD. Oh, we sat . . . and just sat mostly, I guess.

GINGER. Did you go dancing?

HOWARD. Not until she asked me to go to the junior prom.

GINGER. I'll bet you were a wonderful dancer.

HOWARD. I was not. I couldn't dance at all. It took your mother four weeks to teach me a two-step, which we still do.

GINGER. (*Dreaming*) Was the prom fun, Pop?

HOWARD. I remember she led all night.

GINGER. (*Dreaming*) Was it romantic?

HOWARD. Naah, the dance was dull. . . . But . . . (*Chuckles*) I remember that was the night your mother and I got in my old jalopy and drove over to the . . . No, not very romantic.

GINGER. I'd like to have dates and go dancing and sit and just talk.

HOWARD. Is that what's troubling you?

GINGER. Sorta. . . .

HOWARD. You miss seeing Tommy, don't you? (GINGER *rises, crosses R. two steps*) Well, let me tell you something, darling. (HOWARD *rises, crosses R. to Ginger*) Don't let this momentary loneliness keep you from doing anything you want to do. Two to one this separation is much tougher on him than on you.

GINGER. You think so?

HOWARD. Uh-huh.

GINGER. Oh, maybe I better go call him. (*Breaks up toward phone.* HOWARD *stops her*)

HOWARD. No, no. You sit tight and when he does come around you make him accept you, (*Pulling Ginger down to him*) not only as a girl but as anything else you want to be.

GINGER. But suppose he won't accept me as a football player?

HOWARD. Don't you worry. If Tommy is half the boy that you and I know he is, he'll see the justice of your cause, and you'll have a much better time together.

GINGER. All right, Pop. I'll take your word.

HOWARD. Thata girl. Listen to me and you'll learn how to deal with men. (*Crosses down to armchair*)

GINGER. Thanks, Pop.

HOWARD. Feel better? (*Sits in armchair*)

GINGER. Much.

HOWARD. That's good.

GINGER. (*Crosses U. to foot of stairs, stops*) Pop.

HOWARD. Huh?

GINGER. Would you do me a favor?

HOWARD. What, darling?

GINGER. Would you take me to the play tonight? (*Crosses down two steps*) I want to get dressed up and have a date.

HOWARD. I'll be honored.

GINGER. What time will you call for me?

HOWARD. About 8:15.

GINGER. I won't keep you waiting.

HOWARD. You'd better. It's one of the first rules of being a girl.

GINGER. If I do will you be awful mad?

HOWARD. Sore as a boil.

GINGER. It's going to be some date.

HOWARD. We'll make it up over a soda. (AGNES *enters from front door*)

GINGER. (*Backs up R. a step. Blows Howard a kiss*) That's all I can say. (*Crosses up backward to foot of stairs. Collides with Agnes*) Excuse me, Mother.

AGNES. What are you so excited about?

GINGER. I got a date.

AGNES. With whom?

GINGER. A real dream boat. (*Exits up stairs joyously*)

AGNES. (*Crossing D. to C.*) Whom does she have a date with?

HOWARD. Me.

AGNES. (*Crossing L. to Howard*) Well, dream boat, you're really sailing tonight, aren't you?

HOWARD. I certainly am. (AGNES *sits on ottoman*)

AGNES. Hey . . . hey . . . remember when I acted in the senior play?

HOWARD. Yeah, and I rehearsed all the love scenes with you.

AGNES. And most of them weren't in the play. (*Rises. Crossing R. to L. end of sofa*) I'm more excited than Jeannie.

HOWARD. (*Writing on pad he used before*) Every man should be allowed his own faith.

AGNES. What was that?

HOWARD. A faith he can share with his fellow-men.

AGNES. (*Crossing D. to above coffee table*) Howard, please don't write out loud. It makes me nervous.

HOWARD. You know, darling, I think this speech should be eloquent, but terse. Don't you?

AGNES. The terser the better. I'd like to see you keep it under wraps. (*Phone rings*)

HOWARD. In this very precarious situation you're supporting me like a pillar of jello. (*Phone again.* AGNES *crosses U. to answer it*)

AGNES. (*Into phone*) Hello. . . . Yes, she is. Will you hold on for a moment?

GINGER. (*Off*) Mom, was that call for me?

AGNES. No, dear, it's Eddie for Joan. (*Crosses slowly D.R. to L. of sofa*)

GINGER. (*Off*) Oh. . . . Joan, phone.

HOWARD. (*Writing*) "Every man should have a dream and every dream should have a purpose."

AGNES. That's pretty fancy.

HOWARD. Thomas Jefferson said that.

AGNES. (*Crosses D. to sofa*) Well, he wouldn't have if he'd known what it was going to be used for. (*Sits C. of sofa.* JOAN *enters down stairs, dressed for the play. Crosses to phone table, picks up phone*)

JOAN. (*Into phone*) Hi . . . uh-huh . . . sure. . . . (HOWARD *looks up.* JOAN *laughs*) Uh-huh. . . . (HOWARD *echoes her giggle*) Yeah. . . . (HOWARD *listens*) Right. . . . (HOWARD *turns away*) Bye.

HOWARD. (*Chuckles*) That's the least informative telephone conversation I've ever overheard. (JOAN *crosses D. to C.*)

AGNES. She does that all the time.

JOAN. (*To Howard*) Like my dress?

HOWARD. Lovely. Where did you get the talent for such telephone discretion?

JOAN. I'm glad I have talent for something. Mom, will you fix this bow? (*Crosses R. to Agnes. Faces down L.*)

AGNES. (*Fixing bow*) You poor free soul. You're the only completely irresponsible and carefree member of the clan tonight.

JOAN. (*Crossing around to U.L. of sofa*) Well, when Ginger gets as old as I am she'll learn that you either compete with men or go out with them.

AGNES. And what have you decided is the wisest course?

JOAN. Eddie's picking me up in a few minutes.

AGNES. Collaborationist!

JOAN. One of the best there is. I'm going to borrow some of your "Intoxication," Mom. (*Exits up stairs*)

AGNES. Oh, yes. Every once in a while I realize how big that girl is getting. (*Front door bell*) No wonder he's captain of the track team. (*Rises, crosses up to front door*)

HOWARD. He must have phoned from the lawn.

AGNES. (*Off*) Oh, hello. Come in. (AGNES *enters from front door*) It's someone for Virginia. (AGNES *crosses L. to below newel post of stairs.* TOMMY GREEN *enters from front door, stands U.R.*)

HOWARD. Oh, hello, Tommy.

TOMMY. Hello, Mr. Carol.

HOWARD. Come in.

TOMMY. Thank you. (*Crosses down to C.*)

JOAN. (*Off*) Tell him I'll be down in a minute, Mother.

AGNES. It isn't for you.

TOMMY. Is Virginia at home?

AGNES. Yes, she is. Sit down, Tommy. I'll call her. (*Starts R. to go up stairs*)

HOWARD. Just a minute, darling. I'd like to talk to Tommy first.

AGNES. (*Takes step toward Howard*) Dear. . .

HOWARD. Sit down, Tommy. (TOMMY *sits on L. end of sofa*) What do you want to see my daughter about?

TOMMY. Well . . .

AGNES. Darling, it's getting awfully late.

HOWARD. This won't take long.

TOMMY. Well . . .

AGNES. If you two gentlemen will excuse me—(*Crossing L. to kitchen*)—I'm going into the kitchen for no reason. (*Exits into kitchen*)

HOWARD. Well, we got as far as "well" twice.

TOMMY. Mr. Carol, I came here to ask Virginia to the play tonight.

HOWARD. And in asking her, do you think you'll get back in her good graces?

TOMMY. Yes, sir.

HOWARD. How?

TOMMY. I have my whole speech planned. (*Rises. Orates*) "This is not the time to be emotional."

HOWARD. I don't want to hear the whole speech, Tommy.

TOMMY. Oh. Well, the main theme is reason and logic.

HOWARD. (*Rises. Crossing R. to Tommy*) Tommy, I would like to give you some advice out of my rich personal experience. In dealing with women a man must shun reason and logic—(*Pushes Tommy down on L. arm of sofa*)—for time has shown the male of the species has never been able to turn these two weapons to his own advantage. They are the heritage and birthright of the sex, made of gentle steel, who oppose us. Thus every man must forge a weapon of his own design in the fires of this eternal struggle and pray that when he does go to do battle, he will not be reasonably or logically slain more than sixty percent of the time. A simple man can ask no more.

TOMMY. What weapon do you use, sir?

HOWARD. (*Looks up L., then back*) Confusion. In my twenty years of married life I have confused more issues than a liberal, and have emerged the victor over reason, logic, and my wife, forty percent of the time . . . (*Crosses L. to armchair*) I think.

TOMMY. Congratulations.

HOWARD. (*Crosses R., back to Tommy*) As you get older and your duplicity increases, so will your admiration for this—(*As though sprinkling dust over Tommy*)—dust of wisdom I have sprinkled upon you.

TOMMY. Mr. Carol, you mean I should try to confuse Ginger?

HOWARD. No, no. I don't think you'd better try that, Tommy.

TOMMY. If I can't use reason and logic, and I can't use confusion, what's left?

HOWARD. (*Pulls Tommy to his feet*) Action. . . . Dedication. Tommy, at fourteen a woman is impressed by shining knights and holy grails. At eighteen they start to smile indulgently and when they reach my wife's age, they laugh openly. Tommy, if you're going to win Virginia back you've got to prove you're willing to fight for her.

TOMMY. I'm not a fighter, sir.

HOWARD. You can't ask her to that play. You've got to tell her she's going with you.

TOMMY. She'd hit me. (HOWARD *crosses L. to below drum table, then crosses back to Tommy above it*)

HOWARD. You've got to be strong and dominant, yet at the same time you've got to let her know no matter what she is or does, she's your girl.

TOMMY. I'm sorry, sir, but I disagree with you.

HOWARD. You do?

TOMMY. Yes. We've never had to resort to intrigue. Our relationship has always been more mature than that.

HOWARD. (*Crossing up to foot of stairs*) Well, you're the victim. (*Calling up stairs*) Virginia.

GINGER. (*Off*) Yes, Pop?

HOWARD. Will you come down here for a minute? (TOMMY *crosses R. below sofa*)

GINGER. (*Off*) Sure.

HOWARD. (*Crossing L. to drum table*) I'll be sitting right here with pad and pencil—(*Picks up pad and pencil from drum table. Crossing L. to D.L. corner*)—just in case you have any last words for posterity. (HOWARD *turns off wall lamp over D.L. corner, sits on upstage bench, concealed from sight.* GINGER *enters down stairs dressed for play, wearing cape*)

GINGER. (*Coming down*) Yes, Pop. (*On lower landing*) Hello, Tommy.

TOMMY. Hi. . . . (*Crosses up L. two steps*)

GINGER. What do you want?

TOMMY. (*Crosses L. a step*) I came to ask you to the play.

GINGER. You did?

TOMMY. Yes.

GINGER. (*Crossing down stairs to below newel post*) Well, no, thank you.

TOMMY. (*Crossing L. to Ginger*) Why not?

GINGER. Because you're just like every other man. (HOWARD *listens attentively*) You're not big enough in character to accept me as a real equal.

TOMMY. What do you mean?

GINGER. If you recognize me as a football player, then you feel you must discriminate against me as a woman.

TOMMY. Now, just a minute.

GINGER. Don't interrupt. (TOMMY, *exasperated, crosses D. to L. arm of sofa*) I've got six weeks to make up for. (*Crossing D. to L. of Tommy*) I've always liked you because you talked freedom and equality, but when the time came, you couldn't practice it.

TOMMY. I talked about social problems.

GINGER. (*Turns front*) This is a social problem. (*To Tommy*) It's all your fault I'm not accepted as a girl.

TOMMY. My fault?

GINGER. Yes, your fault. If you hadn't been so petty and narrow-minded, you would have taken me out these past six weeks and said, "This is my girl."

TOMMY. (*Front*) "She plays football."

GINGER. Why not?

TOMMY. (*To Ginger*) People laugh.

GINGER. And you're afraid they're laughing at you. You're a coward, Tommy Green.

TOMMY. That's not true.

GINGER. You're passive instead of active—(*Sobs*)—and I never want to see you again! (*Runs up stairs*)

TOMMY. (*Crossing U. to foot of stairs*) All right, if that's the way you feel about it. (*Front door bell*)

HOWARD. How are you doing with reason and logic?

TOMMY. (*Crossing L. to U.R. of part of D.L. corner*) She never gave me a chance. She wants to be both the dominated and dominant figures.

HOWARD. That's because you let her be.

TOMMY. What can I do about it?

HOWARD. I told you. (AGNES *enters from kitchen to answer front door. Crosses R. to U.C.*) The secret of my success with women is that I never let any of them dominate me. (AGNES *stops, looks at Howard, smiles.* HOWARD *looks at her*)

TOMMY. I'm so angry I could go up and drag her down here bodily.

HOWARD. Would you like to try?

EDDIE. (*Off U.R.*) Hya, Mrs. Carol.

AGNES. (*Off U.R.*) Hello, Eddie, come in.

TOMMY. (*Crosses R. to bar*) No. I guess I better go. (AGNES *enters, followed by Eddie Davis, crosses L. to foot of stairs*)

AGNES. I'll get Joan.

EDDIE. Hey, did you hear about the touch-down we set up for your daughter this afternoon?

AGNES. Multiple versions. Excuse me, please. (*Exits up stairs*)

EDDIE. (*Crossing L.*) Hello, Greenie. (*Slaps Tommy on L. shoulder as he passes*) Hya, Mr. Carol. You sure were excited out there on the field today. I thought you were going to have a heart attack. (HOWARD *chokes.* EDDIE *turns R., crosses up to Tommy*) Hey, Greenie, what are you doing here?

TOMMY. Why?

EDDIE. I thought Ginger gave you the brush.

TOMMY. You did.

EDDIE. That's what I heard.

TOMMY. Well, she did. (*Crosses R. to down R. of phone table*)

EDDIE. Oh, I get it. She asked you over to tell you how to lead her cheers next week. (TOMMY *stops below newel post*) Or maybe she invited you to the play, huh?

TOMMY. What does that mean?

EDDIE. (*Crossing R. to below Tommy*) Well, all the guys on the squad are taking their best date, so why shouldn't she take pretty little you? (TOMMY *turns L. and hits Eddie, standing directly down-stage of him, on the jaw.* EDDIE *falls flat between ottoman and L. arm of sofa.* TOMMY *stands with his eyes closed a second, then opens them.* HOWARD *crosses R. to drum table.* GINGER, *carrying cape, enters down stairs, followed by Joan carrying coat, followed by Agnes, who remains on upper landing*)

GINGER. (*Crosses D. to R. of Tommy*) Tommy.

JOAN. (*Crosses down to above armchair*) Eddie.

AGNES. Howard.

HOWARD. Yes, dear?

AGNES. Why didn't you stop them from fighting? *(Crosses down to lower landing)*

HOWARD. Eddie wasn't fighting.

TOMMY. I hate violence.

HOWARD. I can see that.

TOMMY. *(To Ginger)* But some place a man must take an active stand. (EDDIE *rises, crosses suddenly U. to L. of Tommy.* GINGER *steps back to behind L. back of sofa.* AGNES *crosses down stage)*

EDDIE. *(Picks up Tommy's R. fist, looks at it)* You all right? (AGNES *crosses L. to above Howard)*

TOMMY. Fine. (EDDIE *breaks L.*) And from now on, this girl can do whatever she wants to do. She was right and we were all wrong. Is that clear?

EDDIE. Yeah, Tom. . . .

TOMMY. Okay.

JOAN. *(Turns L. to Howard and Agnes)* So long, Mom. . . . *(Kisses Agnes)* . . . Dad. *(Kisses Howard over Agnes' L. shoulder)*

HOWARD. Night, Joan.

AGNES. Have a good time, Joan.

JOAN. Yeah. *(Turns to Eddie, who reaches for her coat, which she does not give him)* You coming, athlete?

EDDIE. Well, yes dear, I am. (JOAN *exits to front door.* EDDIE *shrugs, smiles, follows her off*)

TOMMY. Well, good night, Mrs. Carol. . . . Mr. Carol (*To Ginger*) What I wanted to say before was that I am sorry about the way I acted the past six weeks.

GINGER. (*Crossing L. to Tommy*) Tommy Green, aren't you going to ask me to the play?

TOMMY. I did ask you.

GINGER. Don't you want to ask me again?

TOMMY. All right. Want to go to the play with me?

GINGER. Sure. (*Hands Tommy cape. He puts it on her. Crossing L. to Agnes*) I'm ready if you are, Tommy.

TOMMY. Okay, let's go.

AGNES. (*Crossing R. to Ginger*) Have a nice time, Virginia.

TOMMY. Night, Mrs. Carol. (*Crosses L. to Howard. Extends R. hand*) Thanks, Dad. (HOWARD *crosses up away from Tommy, considers a moment, then crosses down to Tommy, shakes his hand*)

HOWARD. All right, son.

TOMMY. (*Crossing R. to below Ginger*) Come on, Virginia, let's go.

HOWARD. Oh, Tommy. . . . (TOMMY *and* GINGER *stop*) Can I have a minute alone with your girl?

TOMMY. (*Looks at his wrist-watch*) It's getting pretty late.

AGNES. (*Crossing R. to Tommy, takes Tommy by arm*) Come along, Mr. Green. I'd like to know your intentions. (AGNES *and* TOMMY *exit to front door*)

HOWARD. I just had to tell you, you're very beautiful, little girl.

GINGER. Thanks, Pop. Oh, I'm sorry I had to break our date.

HOWARD. (*Crossing R. to Ginger*) I understand.

GINGER. (*Looks over to window R. and back*) You were right about Tommy.

HOWARD. What do you mean?

GINGER. You said he'd come back, and he did.

HOWARD. I only knew that because that's what *I* always did.

GINGER. And you said he'd accept me for what I am.

HOWARD. He had no other choice. (*Crossing D. to L. of sofa with Ginger, who sits C. on sofa*) You know, I may have been right about Tommy, but there was something I was very wrong about. (*Sits on L. end of sofa*)

GINGER. What?

HOWARD. You and me.

GINGER. What do you mean, Pop?

HOWARD. When you said to Tommy a little while ago, "You're just like every other man," you meant me, didn't you?

GINGER. No, Pop.

HOWARD. Oh, yes, you did. I certainly made an unholy spectacle of myself this afternoon, didn't I?

GINGER. (*Laughs*) Sort of.

HOWARD. Yeah, but there were a lot of reasons for it. First of all, when I saw you run out on the field I didn't care what anybody thought. I had a football player in the family. You see . . . and this is a secret, just between us and your mother . . . when I was in high school I wasn't a very good football player. (*Sits back*) As a matter of fact, I never got into any of the games.

GINGER. You didn't?

HOWARD. No, so this was my first game, as well as yours. You know, when I heard the coach say, "Send Carol in," I almost ran out onto the field myself. (GINGER *laughs, then becomes serious*)

GINGER. Pop?

HOWARD. What, darling?

GINGER. Are you sorry I'm not a boy?

HOWARD. I wouldn't trade you for any boy in the world. (HOWARD *embraces Ginger, with her head over his R. shoulder*)

GINGER. May I tell you a secret now, Pop?

HOWARD. You sure can. (HOWARD *breaks embrace*)

GINGER. Being a girl is so much fun, I've decided to give up football. (HOWARD *releases Ginger, turns L.*)

HOWARD. Is that what you want to do most in the world, Miss Carol?

GINGER. Yes, Daddy.

HOWARD. All right. (GINGER *rises, picks up her bag and gloves from coffee table*)

GINGER. Oh, can I always tell you my secrets?

HOWARD. I hope you will, but I know you won't.

GINGER. Why not?

HOWARD. Because today I'm the man you love, but one of these days I'll just be your father.

TOMMY. (*Off*) Virginia. (GINGER *crosses R. to window, looks out. She looks back to Howard, who smiles and nods at her. She crosses L. above sofa to U.C., and stands facing Howard while she fixes her dress. He looks at her once more, and she exits to front door, stepping off with a determined stride.* HOWARD *rises, crosses up to 'Life' picture on wall, takes it down. He looks at it a moment, then places it face down on chair R. of sideboard. Crosses to D.L. corner, picks up his pad from bench*)

HOWARD. (*Reading*) "Every man should have a dream, and every dream should have a purpose." (*Crossing R. to drum table*) Thomas Jefferson. (*Tears speech off pad, crumbles it, puts it on table*) No wonder he died broke! (*Crosses U. around armchair, sits. Picks up contracts, signs them with a pen from tray on drum table*)

GINGER. (*Off*) Good night, Mom.

TOMMY. (*Off*) Good night, Mrs. Carol.

AGNES. (*Off*) Have fun, kids. (AGNES *enters from front door*) Ed and Phyllis are waiting for us out front in the car, Howard. (*Gets her cape, bag and gloves from chair R. of phone table, puts cape on*)

HOWARD. All right.

AGNES. You ready?

HOWARD. In a minute.

AGNES. Howard, will you please stop writing that speech?

HOWARD. I'm not writing any speech. I'm signing the contracts for the bank.

AGNES. (*Turns L.*) What? When did that happen?

HOWARD. Just now.

AGNES. But why? How?

HOWARD. Agnes, come here.

AGNES. We haven't got much time

HOWARD. No, no. I want to ask you something. (AGNES *crosses L. to R. of ottoman*) When did you buy that dress for Virginia?

AGNES. When the season began. I thought she'd need it.

HOWARD. You did, huh?

AGNES. Yes.

HOWARD. She certainly is a little girl now.

AGNES. (*Looking R.*) She certainly is. Howard, I've got a wonderful idea.

HOWARD. What?

AGNES. (*Crossing R. to down C.*) It's something I've been thinking about for a long time.

HOWARD. What?

AGNES. Why don't you and I have a son, huh? (HOWARD *laughs, rises, crosses to Agnes, takes her in his arms*)

HOWARD. Say, do we really have to go to that play tonight?

AGNES. Howard! (*They cross U. toward front door as*)

CURTAIN FALLS

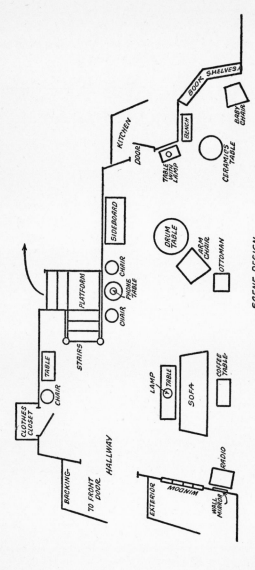

SCENE DESIGN

"TIME OUT FOR GINGER"

PROPERTY LIST

On Stage, at rise, Act I:

Radio console, D.R.
  Bowl of flowers on console
Small framed mirror on wall over console
Drapes on window
Curtains on window
Sofa
  2 pillows on sofa
  1 curtain unfolded over R. side of back of sofa
1 curtain, unfolded, on floor D.R. sofa
Coffee table D.S. sofa
Table behind sofa
  Magazines
Table S.R. arch
  Lamp
Picture on wall over table
Table in hallway, R. stairway
  Vase of flowers
Hallway chair, S.R. table
Chair, R. of phone table
Phone table, below lower staircase landing
  Telephone
  Vase of flowers
Chair R. of sideboard
Sideboard
Small table D.S. kitchen door
  Framed family photographs
In D.L. corner
  Cushions on bench
  Small chair

Table
Small potter's wheel
Baked, unglazed ceramic—small pitcher or bowl on potter's wheel
   Small rack containing poster paint bottles, with 1 place unfilled
   Small glass containing paint-brushes
Small pictures on D.L. wall
Bookcase over bench, D.L. corner
Armchair, L.C.
Table, L. armchair
Small platter with 3 sharpened pencils and fountain pen, filled
Ottoman, R. armchair
In Hallway Closet
   Old hats
   Galoshes and Rubbers

Off R.:

For HOWARD:
   Typed speech
   Brief case
      Act I
         ¼ pound jelly beans in paper bag
         Time magazine
         Banking papers in folder
      Act II, scene 1
         ¼ pound jelly beans in paper bag
         Special *Life* magazine
   Small piece goalpost—Act II, Scene 2
   Bunch of keys in case—Act III
   Corsage in box—Act III
For AGNES:
   2 empty stocking boxes, wrapped and tied—Act I
   Cardboard box containing jar of poster paint, tied to open
      easily—Act I
   1 section full-sized newspaper—Act I
   Black bag and gloves—Act I
For GINGER:
   School books—Act I
   Football pants, stuffed with jersey, shoulder pads and helmet—
      Act I

For JEANNIE:
   School books—Act I
   1 petition, folded—Act I
For JOAN:
   1 petition, folded—Act II, Scene 1
   2 mail sacks—Act II, Scene 2
For EDDIE:
   1 typed list—Act I
For WILSON:
   1 petition, folded—Act I
For HOFFMAN:
   3 contracts, folded—Act III

To be preset, Act II, Scene 1:

   1 blue bowl
   2 books

To be preset, Act II, Scene 2:

Framed *Life* cover, on wall over sideboard
Shopping bag, against L. side coffee table, with several bundles of
   mail, scattered on coffee table

To be preset, Act III:

Pitcher of flowers on sideboard
Agnes' evening wrap, bag and gloves, on chair R. of phone table

Off L.:

For AGNES:
   Small towel, wrapped around nail buffer and empty nail cream
     jar—Act III
For HOWARD—*Act III:*
   1 Petticoat on hanger
   Joan's evening dress on hanger
For GINGER:
   Glass of milk—Act I
   Raw carrot—Act I

For LIZ:
    Coffee service—Act I
      tray
      coffee pot filled with coffee
      2 cups and saucers
    Wicker sewing basket—Act I
    1 coke—Act I
    Special *Life* magazine—Act II, Scene 1
For JOAN:
    1 coke—Act II, Scene 1
    1 coke—Act II, Scene 2
    Laundry bundle, Act II, Scene 2
    Hair brush—Act III
For JEANNIE:
    1 coke—Act II, Scene 2

To be Preset, Act II, Scene 2:

30-odd packets of letters and telegrams, scattered on D.L. bench and drum table

To be preset, Act III:

Legal size yellow pad of paper, on L.C. table
New ceramic—small pitcher or jar on potter's wheel

PROPERTY PLOT

Act I:

As indicated in property list

Act II, Scene 1:

Strike:
    Ceramic from potter's wheel on the ceramic table
    Brief-case from L. wall table

Glass from drum table
Petition from drum table
Time magazine from drum table
Newspaper from drum table
Cup and saucer from drum table
Coffee service from coffee table
Cup and saucer from coffee table
Jelly beans from chair R. of the sideboard
Flowers from phone table

Set:
Move ceramic table against the downstage bench
Special *Life* magazine in brief-case, off R.
Jelly beans in brief-case, off R.
2 books on console

Act II, Scene 2:

Strike:
Brief-case from L. wall table
Coke bottle from coffee table
Life magazine from coffee table
Glass from drum table

Set:
Shopping bag, against L. side of coffee table
18 packets of mail scattered on coffee table
Hang framed *Life* picture on wall over sideboard
Scatter 36 packets of mail on bench in D.L. corner and on drum
    table

Act III:

Strike:
Mail from inside bench
Shopping bag from platform
Mail bags from below phone table
Piece of goal-post from coffee table
2 books from console

Set:

Unscrew caps of red and blue paint jars in rack, in D.L. corner
New ceramic on potter's wheel
Pad on drum table
Agnes' evening wrap, bag and gloves on chair R. of phone table
Petticoat and Joan's Act III dress on hanger off L.